A novelization by Jordan Horowitz
From the screenplay by John Hughes
Based on the characters
created by Hank Ketcham

SCHOLASTIC INC.
New York Toronto London Auckland Sydney

WARNER BROS. PRESENTS

A JOHN HUGHES PRODUCTION A NICK CASTLE FILM "DENNIS THE MENACE" CHRISTOPHER LLOYD
JOAN PLOWRIGHT LEA THOMPSON PAUL WINFIELD MASON GAMBLE AND WALTER MATTHAU AS MR. WILSON
MUSIC BY JERRY GOLDSMITH FILM EDITOR ALAN HEIM A.C.E. PRODUCTION DESIGNER JAMES BISSELL DIRECTOR OF PHOTOGRAPHY THOMAS ACKERMAN EXECUTIVE PRODUCER ERNEST CHAMBERS
WRITTEN BY JOHN HUGHES BASED ON CHARACTERS CREATED BY HANK KETCHAM PRODUCED BY JOHN HUGHES AND RICHARD VANE DIRECTED BY NICK CASTLE

ISBN 0-590-47350-6

12 11 10 9 8 7 6 5 4 3 2   3 4 5 6 7 8/9

Printed in the U.S.A.   40

First Scholastic printing, June 1993

Contents

1.
School's Out

Cats scattered and headed for cover.

Squirrels scampered hurriedly up a tree.

A gopher squirted down his hole.

Even an army of ants retreated into its nest.

They were all running away from the same thing, a little freckle-faced boy in overalls who, at that very moment, was pedaling his way down the street on his bicycle. He had blond hair with a cowlick that stood so straight up from the back of his head that it seemed to defy the breeze that whisked against it. His name was Dennis Mitchell and he was riding down the street pulling a wagon filled with junk. Although he was a small boy of only five years old, he was already famous for some big things.

Big disasters.

Big messes.

Big trouble.

That was why when the milkman saw Dennis, he jumped back into his truck and roared away.

And when two sewage workers heard the squeaky sound of Dennis's bicycle, they jumped down into their manhole and covered it with the lid.

And when a teenage girl who had been hanging her laundry on a line saw Dennis pedal by, she quickly grabbed all of her wash and ran back inside her house.

It was a quiet Monday morning. The first Monday since the school year had ended. Dennis had gotten up early that morning and had taken his wagon out on a junk-finding expedition.

When he had loaded the wagon with all the important junk he needed, including a tree branch, a tattered teddy bear, a piece of bubble gum wrap, and a garter snake, he decided to pay a visit to his neighbor Mr. Wilson.

George and Martha Wilson had lived next door to the Mitchells for as long as Dennis could remember, which wasn't very long to begin with. Although Mr. Wilson was old enough to be his grandfather, Dennis liked him just as if he were a friend his own age. It didn't matter to Dennis that sometimes Mr. Wilson got mad at him. Part of being a good friend meant being able to forgive someone when they made a mistake, and Dennis always forgave Mr. Wilson for getting mad. Besides, no matter how often George Wilson got mad at him, Martha never did. So Dennis felt welcome to bring his bicycle to a screeching halt right under the Wilsons' kitchen window.

"HEY! MR. WILSON!" Dennis screamed so loud that his cowlick shook.

From behind the kitchen door Mr. Wilson peeked through a lace curtain. It was so early, he was still dressed in his pajamas and bathrobe. Dennis had climbed down from his bicycle and was now making his way to the back porch. What was more, Dennis's shaggy sheepdog, Ruff, was following right behind.

"Holy smokes! He's comin' in!" Mr. Wilson said in a panic.

Today of all days Mr. Wilson did not want to be bothered by Dennis Mitchell's mischief. Today was the day that the Garden Club selection committee was going to announce that the annual flower show would be held in his garden. Mr. Wilson was very proud of his garden. And he was especially proud of his Night Blooming Mock Orchid, which he had been growing for many years. It was a special kind of plant that takes forty years to blossom. And once it opens, it withers in a matter of minutes. Mr. Wilson was hoping that his Night Blooming Mock Orchid would be the main attraction at the flower show. And with all his excitement, he did not want Dennis coming around and ruining his good spirits.

But a second later Mr. Wilson could hear Dennis

knocking at the door. He quickly turned, wheeled out of the kitchen, ran through the dining room, and started upstairs. His wife, Martha, who was coming down the stairs to answer the door, had to squeeze against the wall so as not to get in his way.

"George!" exclaimed Martha. "What on earth — ?"

"Stand away, Martha," said Mr. Wilson hurriedly. "Dennis Mitchell is outside. Tell him I'm sick!"

"I won't fib for you, George," said his wife. She was a very honest person.

"He's out of school for the summer," begged Mr. Wilson. "If you let him in now, he'll be here for months! We won't get a moment of peace!"

Martha continued down the stairs. "If this house gets any more peaceful, George," she said, "the mice'll get bored and leave."

"Martha! I'm begging you!" pleaded Mr. Wilson just before he ran the rest of the way up the stairs and into his bedroom. Once there he went into his bathroom and pulled down all the medicine bottles he could find. Then he began arranging them on the night table next to his bed.

If Dennis Mitchell got past Martha and made it upstairs, Mr. Wilson wanted to make sure it looked like he was really sick.

4

2.
Doctor Dennis

As soon as the back door opened, Dennis looked up and saw Martha's warm, smiling face looking down at him.

"Hi, Mrs. Wilson," Dennis said cheerfully. "Is Mr. Wilson here? I don't have to go back to school until I'm six. I wanted to tell him that I can see him all the time now, not just after school and on Saturdays and Sundays and holidays and when I'm home with the flubug."

"Mr. Wilson's upstairs, dear," said Martha in her kindly voice.

"Can I go up and see him, or is he in the bathroom reading the newspaper?" asked Dennis.

"I'm not sure Mr. Wilson wants to see anyone right now," answered Martha. She was not exactly sure *what* to tell Dennis.

"Is he bare naked?"

"No, Dennis." Martha blushed.

"Does he got his teeth out?"

"No dear. He's — "

"Sleeping?"

"Yes, dear. He's sleeping." Martha nodded.

"Doesn't he get up real, real, real early?" asked Dennis.

"Usually."

"Does he got an alarm clock?"

"Yes."

"Is it broke?"

"No."

"How come it didn't wake him up?"

Martha was not sure what to say. Dennis was such a clever little boy. It was one of the reasons she liked him so much.

"Maybe he didn't hear it," she suggested.

Dennis thought about that. "You know what, Mrs. Wilson?" he asked after a moment.

"What?" replied Martha.

"I think Mr. Wilson wants to be awake, but he doesn't know it because he's sleeping," explained Dennis. "And you know what I do when my dad is sleeping and he doesn't want to?"

Martha looked at Dennis suspiciously. "What?" she asked cautiously.

Dennis grabbed the door, took one giant step back, and slammed it shut.

The sound of the loud slam traveled all the way up to the bedroom where Mr. Wilson was still arranging medicine bottles on his night table. As soon as Mr. Wilson heard the door slam, he knew that Dennis was inside the house. He quickly jumped into bed and under the covers, bathrobe and all.

Downstairs Dennis stood proudly in the Wilsons' kitchen.

"I bet Mr. Wilson's wide awake now," he said to Martha. "No grown-up person can sleep when somebody does something like that to their door. It chips the paint and makes the hinges loose."

Martha didn't know what to say. She knew that her husband was in no mood to be bothered by Dennis, but she didn't have the heart to turn the boy away.

Within minutes Dennis was carefully climbing up the stairs, squeaking the floorboards with each step. When he reached the landing, he went to the Wilsons' bedroom door and peeked in. He could see the bed where Mr. Wilson lay. Mr. Wilson's eyes were closed, but his mouth was wide open, letting out long, regular snores.

Dennis crept into the room and tiptoed right up to the bed. When he saw the rows of medicine bottles on the night table, he let out a soft whistle of amazement.

"Poor old Mr. Wilson must be real sick," he said quietly so as not to wake his friend. "No wonder he ain't up."

Dennis leaned in closer and examined Mr. Wilson's face. He didn't know that Mr. Wilson was really wide awake and looking at him through his eyelashes.

"Yikes!" said Dennis. "His skin looks like old, wrinkled-up dead leaves."

Next, Dennis placed his head on Mr. Wilson's chest and listened to his heart.

"Wow!" he exclaimed in a whisper. "His heart sounds like our washing machine."

Dennis decided to give Mr. Wilson a full medical examination right then and there. He took out the little flashlight he always carried for junk-hunting and shined it around Mr. Wilson's mouth.

"His tongue's very ugly and blue and spotty," he noticed. Then he aimed the flashlight beam up into Mr. Wilson's nose and took in the view.

"Cool!" he said.

Finally, Dennis placed his small hand on Mr. Wilson's forehead. That was exactly what his own mother did when he felt sick.

"Uh-oh. He feels warm," said Dennis. "I better take his temperature."

Dennis went into Mr. Wilson's bathroom and opened the medicine chest. He saw a thermometer way up on the third shelf. He had to raise himself up on his toes and stretch his fingers to reach for it. He had just managed to touch the thermometer with his fingertips when it rolled forward and flipped off the shelf . . .

. . . out of the medicine cabinet . . .

. . . and into the toilet bowl. *Splash!*

In the bedroom Mr. Wilson cringed at the sound of the splash. He leaned over the side of the bed and tried to see into the bathroom. But all he could see was Dennis wearing a rubber cleaning glove and fishing something out of the toilet bowl.

Mr. Wilson could only imagine what mischief Dennis Mitchell was causing in his bathroom. Still, he could not let on that he was awake. Otherwise the boy might end up staying for the rest of the day. And that would make him feel really sick.

By the time Dennis had pulled the thermometer out of the toilet, it was dripping wet. As he went back into the bedroom he began to shake the thermometer down the same way he had seen his mother do many times. But the thermometer was so slippery, it flew from his hand and onto the floor where it shattered to bits.

"Shoot," exclaimed Dennis. He wondered what he could do now to help poor old sick Mr. Wilson. "He doesn't need his temperature took," he thought aloud. "He's hot enough. He needs a aspirin."

Dennis plucked a bottle of aspirin off the night table and looked at the label. It read:

FOR FAST, EFFECTIVE RELIEF
OF PAIN AND FEVER. THE BRAND
DOCTORS RECOMMEND MOST.

This was just what Mr. Wilson needed, thought Dennis as he unscrewed the lid of the bottle. But when he tried to empty some aspirin into his hand, nothing came out. A wad of cotton was stuffed in the opening. So Dennis shook the bottle. Suddenly the wad of cotton popped out of the bottle followed by about a hundred aspirin tablets. Pretty soon the tablets were all bouncing and tinkling across the wood floor.

Dennis scrambled to pick up an aspirin from the floor. When he caught one, he blew the dust off it and wiped it on his overalls.

When he was sure the aspirin was clean, Dennis climbed onto the bed and sat on Mr. Wilson's belly. It was the only way he could think of to feed the aspirin to Mr. Wilson without waking him up. But when he reached over to drop the aspirin into Mr. Wilson's mouth, Mr. Wilson's mouth suddenly snapped closed. No matter how many times he tried, Dennis couldn't get the aspirin down Mr. Wilson's throat.

Dennis was losing his patience. How would Mr. Wilson get better if he couldn't take his aspirin? Reaching into his back pocket, he pulled out his slingshot. He had been practicing his aim lately, and now all that practicing would have to pay off.

He loaded the aspirin into the rubber band and pulled it back through the cradle of the slingshot.

Then he aimed the slingshot over Mr. Wilson's mouth.

He held the rubber band tightly and waited until Mr. Wilson opened his lips to take a breath.

Then, *twang!* He fired the aspirin into Mr. Wilson's mouth.

Gag! Spit! Mr. Wilson did not like that very much. A minute later he threw Dennis off of his bed and chased him down the stairs, through the living room, and out the front door.

3.
Morning with the Mitchells

Dennis's parents were having breakfast when Dennis barged in through the back door.

"Where have you been?" asked his father, Henry.

"I was at Mr. Wilson's house," explained Dennis breathlessly. "And boy is he ever sick. He has a fever. He's burnin' up!"

Dennis's mother, Alice, grew concerned. She knew that whenever Dennis paid a visit on Mr. Wilson it usually made their neighbor very upset. She went to the telephone and called Martha to see if everything was all right. But when she got off the phone Dennis could tell she was angry.

"Did you shoot an aspirin in Mr. Wilson's mouth with a slingshot?" asked Alice, her arms folded sternly across her chest.

"I didn't want him to bite my fingers off with those big fake teeth," explained Dennis. "Those things are sharp!"

"Mr. Wilson is very angry with you," said Alice.

12

"I thought he was sick," Dennis insisted. "I was just trying to help!"

"He didn't ask for your help and he didn't invite you to his house at six-thirty in the morning," said Alice.

"Nobody invites people to their house at six-thirty in the morning, for gosh sakes," Dennis answered back.

Henry was starting to get fed up with Dennis. "You go sit in the corner and think about what you did," he ordered.

"For how long?" asked Dennis.

"Until you're sorry," replied Henry.

Dennis smiled. "Oh, good," he said smartly. "I'm sorry now."

"He can't sit in the corner, Henry," Alice interrupted. "I have to drop him off at Margaret Wade's house."

Dennis screamed in alarm. Margaret Wade was a little girl Dennis's own age. Her idea of having fun was playing house. That meant playing with dolls and stuff. Dennis wondered: was this some kind of punishment for making Mr. Wilson angry?

"I didn't do anything bad enough to have to go to Margaret's house," Dennis insisted as he watched his mother finish her breakfast. "She's a man-eater," he continued, hoping he could change his mother's mind. "She tortures me. She's mean. She's ugly. She doesn't share!"

"I made arrangements with Mrs. Wade for you

to go to their house when I work," replied Alice. She had just started a new job, the first she had taken since Dennis was born. Now both she and Henry would be away during the weekdays.

"Are you *serious?*" Dennis exclaimed.

"You can't spend the summer unsupervised," explained Alice. "You're out of school."

"I'll go back!"

"Your mother made arrangements," said Henry in a firm voice. "I don't want any arguments."

Dennis sat helplessly at the breakfast table. It was two against one. Dennis knew he had no chance against those odds. He slumped forward and let his forehead drop on the table with a thud.

"My life is falling part," he said miserably.

Before Henry Mitchell left for work he took possession of the infamous slingshot Dennis had used to feed Mr. Wilson the aspirin. Although he did not approve of his son's knack for causing mischief, he had to smile at Dennis's cleverness. A slingshot, he thought with a smile. That was certainly *one* way to get the medicine down.

As he started his car, Henry could see next door where Mr. Wilson was pulling Dennis's bike and wagon down his driveway. Henry decided to walk over and talk with Mr. Wilson. An apology never hurt where Dennis was concerned.

"Hello, George," he said. "Sorry about this morning."

14

Mr. Wilson was not smiling. In fact, his face was still red with anger. "I'm not going to mince words, Henry," he said sternly. He was wiping some gooey stickiness from the bicycle's handlebars off his hands with his handkerchief. "Your kid is driving me nuts."

"I've talked to him. I'll talk to him again."

"Maybe it isn't talk that he needs," growled Mr. Wilson. "When my old man had something important to tell me, he told me with his belt."

"That's not how I deal with my son, Mr. Wilson," said Henry. He could never imagine hitting Dennis no matter how much trouble he caused.

"Well, however you're dealing with him," began Mr. Wilson, "he hasn't learned it's not good manners to break in on a fella and shoot an aspirin down his throat."

"Mr. Wilson, he's only five."

"When I was five I had some respect."

"If you did you were probably a pretty exceptional boy," said Henry.

"In 1925 I wasn't the exception," said Mr. Wilson. "I was the rule."

"I'm running late," said Henry looking at his watch. "I'll make sure Dennis doesn't come by anymore."

"Careful how you say it," cautioned Mr. Wilson. "I don't want everybody in the neighborhood to think I'm a child hater or an ogre. I'm a reasonable man who expects reasonable treatment from his neighbors and their children. I was with the post office for forty years — "

"I'm running a little late," interrupted Henry. "If you'd like, I can come by after work and continue the conversation."

"There's nothing to continue," replied Mr. Wilson. "I've said my piece. We'll leave it at that. The boy can't come over here unless he's gonna behave himself."

"He won't be over at all," promised Henry as he started back toward his car.

"Don't make me out to be a grump," Mr. Wilson called out. "I didn't say never."

"I really have to go," Henry said as he opened his car door.

"He busted my thermometer!" called Mr. Wilson. "It was brand new."

"I'll replace it this afternoon," Henry called back.

"That's not the point!" insisted Mr. Wilson.

"Have a nice day," called Henry as he started his car.

"He's out of school now," shouted Mr. Wilson as Henry drove off. "He can't spend all his free time here. I'm not the bad guy in this, Mitchell. I'm the victim!"

Martha came out of the house when she heard her husband's shouting voice. She could see Henry pulling away down the street in his car.

16

"George? Who are you shouting at?" she asked her husband.

"Mitchell," said Mr. Wilson. "And I wasn't shouting. I was making my point. It's not right that that youngster can run wild, doing what he pleases without regard to people or property."

"He's only a boy, George."

Mr. Wilson glanced over at Dennis's house. "He's gonna knot my rope once too often. I can't take that kid. He's a menace!"

"How do you feel about me working?" Alice Mitchell asked Dennis as she drove their station wagon to the Wades' house.

Dennis remained quietly buckled in his seat belt and did not answer his mother. It was the first time he would be away from her when school was out. And he did not like the idea at all.

"You don't like it, huh?" said Alice. Again Dennis did not respond. "I'm not sure *I* like it," she continued. "What do you think about that?"

Dennis looked up at his mother with surprise. He wondered why she had to go to work if she didn't like leaving him with someone else. Somehow Alice sensed what he was thinking.

"To live the way we're used to," she explained, "I need to work. A lot of moms work. And the best I could do finding someone to watch you is make an arrangement with Mrs. Wade."

"What about Joey?" Dennis asked. He was thinking about the little boy who was his best friend in the whole world. "Did you think about that? What if he comes over? He'll think I moved."

"He won't come over," said Alice.

"Wanna bet?"

"Sure. I'll bet you a quarter."

Dennis smirked. "What can that buy?"

"Not much," answered Alice.

"Okay," agreed Dennis. He and Alice shook hands on the bet.

"You want to pay me now?" asked Alice after a pause.

Dennis was confused. "You don't pay until the bet's over," he said.

"The bet's over," said Alice.

"No, it's not!"

"Yes it is," Alice insisted. "You see, Joey's mother made plans with Mrs. Wade just like I did. Joey is at Margaret's house."

Dennis was puzzled for a moment. Then he realized his mother had tricked him. She knew all along that Joey would be at Margaret's house. Suddenly Dennis felt much better. Margaret didn't stand a chance against him and Joey.

4.
A Visit with Margaret

Margaret and Joey were facing off in the back yard when they heard the Mitchells' station wagon pull into the driveway.

"Do it!" Margaret commanded Joey. Then she puckered her lips and waited for a kiss.

But Joey just sat across from her at the picnic table and shook his head.

By now Margaret was losing her patience. She was tall for her age, much taller than Joey. And when she gave an order she expected it to be carried out.

"I can make you," warned Margaret.

"How?" asked Joey, daring her.

Margaret set her ratty old baby doll on the table and made a fist. But Joey was not intimidated.

"No," he said, steadfastly refusing.

"Then I'll slug your face," threatened Margaret.

"I'll slug you back," said Joey.

"You can't hit a girl!"

"I can, too!"

"Try it," dared Margaret. "I'll scream so awfully and bloody deadly terrible that my mom'll think you tried to murder me. And I'll tell her you did and she'll believe me because boys are like that and girls aren't."

It was a dirty trick. "That stinks," said Joey.

"So do fish and there's nothing you can do about it," said Margaret. "So quit wasting time. Moosh your lips together and let's get this over with."

Joey realized that he had no choice. That's what you get when you're forced to play with girls. All they ever want to do is play house and smooch. *Yucch!* He forced himself to pucker his lips.

"Close your eyes!" Margaret ordered.

"Why?"

"I don't want to get your slimy, gross eyeball juice on my glasses."

Joey reluctantly closed his eyes. The sooner he got this over with the better. Besides, soon Dennis would be there and then Margaret Wade would see who was boss.

"Kiss me!" said Margaret.

Joey moved his face across the picnic table and bravely planted his lips on Margaret. But something felt funny. He did not feel Margaret's lips against his, even though he had no idea what a girl's lips might feel like. He was just certain that these were not Margaret's lips.

And when he opened his eyes he saw that he was right. Instead of her lips, Margaret had placed the bare bottom of her baby doll in front of his face.

"Sucker!" she laughed. Then she got up and ran into her house.

Joey sat red-faced and fuming at the picnic table. He had heard the car pull up minutes ago. Why was it taking Dennis so long to come outside?

What was taking so long was the fact that no matter how hard his mother pleaded with him, Dennis simply refused to be stuck with Margaret for a whole day. Eventually Alice gave up asking, grabbed Dennis by the arm, and began pulling him up the walkway to the Wades' front door. Mrs. Wade was standing in the doorway waiting for them.

"Penny! Hi!" said Alice to Mrs. Wade with an embarrassed smile on her face. The heels of Dennis's high-tops were scraping against the concrete lane.

"Having a problem?" asked Mrs. Wade with a self-satisfied grin on her face. Alice knew that Mrs. Wade was enjoying watching her struggle with Dennis. Mrs. Wade liked to boast about how *her* little Margaret was so perfectly well-behaved and good-mannered. Alice wished that Dennis could be more like Margaret sometimes. Especially when they were out in public.

"He's not happy with the arrangement," said Alice as she and Dennis approached the doorstep.

21

"You need to explain it to him," Mrs. Wade said calmly. She felt she was an expert in dealing with small children. "Kids need to understand a situation just like big people do."

Mrs. Wade knelt beside Dennis. "Dennis, honey? Hi." Her voice was so sweet that it made Dennis a little nauseated. "You know what? Mrs. Wade needs a favor from you."

Mrs. Wade looked up at Alice. "You don't need to hold his arm, Alice," she smiled. "We'll talk this through. He has to learn that children are treated like children when they behave like children."

Some nerve, thought Alice as she let go of Dennis's arm. She felt insulted that Mrs. Wade thought she could handle Dennis better, only Alice was too polite to say so.

"Dennis?" said Mrs. Wade. "I respect you and your feelings." She was certain Dennis would understand the need for good behavior and go peacefully into the house.

WRONG! Seconds later it was Alice who was helping Mrs. Wade drag Dennis through the front door and into the living room. And the only way to keep him there was to pin him down on the floor.

Mrs. Wade smiled weakly as she struggled to keep Dennis down on the floor. "I think we broke through," she remarked, not wanting to admit failure. "Right, Dennis?"

Mrs. Wade looked slightly embarrassed as she

smiled at Alice. Alice could only return her look with one of sympathy.

The first thing Margaret did after she joined Dennis and Joey in the back yard was to go down the list of activities she had planned for them. Since they were her guests, she wanted to be the most perfect hostess that she could be. Just the same as her mother was when PTA meetings were held at their house.

But as soon as she went down her list of fun things to do, like washing her doll's outfits and preparing make-believe tea and cakes, Dennis and Joey looked at each other with sour faces. Then they climbed up one of Mrs. Wade's apple trees and nestled themselves safely in the branches away from Margaret. They knew Margaret wouldn't climb up after them because her mother always made her wear dresses instead of blue jeans.

"This isn't fair!" she shouted up at the boys.

"It's not my fault you wear dumb dresses and doll shoes," Dennis called back.

"It's not my fault, either," added Joey.

Margaret angrily placed her hands on her hips. "You guys are the boring ones," she said. "There's lots to do."

"Oh, really?" asked Dennis. "Like what? Wash dolls?"

"I have hundreds of toys," answered Margaret.

"Your toys are all soft and pink and harmless and safe," said Dennis.

Margaret paused for a moment. What could she think of that the boys would want to do? "We don't have to play with toys," she said. "We can practice singing songs. We could put on a play or a puppet show."

"We could bury you alive!" said Joey gleefully.

"I could pound your face!" replied Margaret. Now she was getting mad.

"It doesn't matter anyway, Margaret," said Dennis. "We're leaving pretty soon. We have work to do."

Margaret was confused. "You can't leave," she told the boys. "My mother's watching you. And you're lying because what work would you have to do?"

"We're gonna make a fort," said Joey.

"Get lost," said Margaret. She did not believe them one bit. They would say anything to get out of playing with her.

"We're going to Turley's Woods," explained Dennis. "There's a fort there that we're gonna take over and fix up."

Margaret tightened her lips. "If you're going there, you have to take me," she said. "Sorry!"

"Not on your life," said Dennis with alarm. "Then you'd know where it is and you'd come over all the time."

But Margaret knew exactly what to do to get

her way with Dennis and Joey. "You can't leave unless I go with you, or I'll tell on you," she told them. "So tough kitty paws, I'm going. Climb down from there. I'll go get my purse."

Dennis and Joey looked at each other and sighed again. They felt defeated. Somehow bringing a purse to a fort building did not seem like much fun.

Turley's Woods was a small area close enough to the children's neighborhood to be safe, but far enough away to be a good hideaway. The last time Dennis and Joey snuck off to play there they had come upon an old tree house that was hidden from view.

"That thing's been there our whole life and we never knew it," said Dennis as he pointed out the tree house to Margaret.

"Do you think anybody lives in it?" asked Joey.

"Just squirrels and birds," answered Dennis.

"Who's it belong to?" asked Margaret.

"It's pretty old," said Dennis. "The guy who owned it probably grew up and died. I don't know anybody who says it belongs to them, so I think it's okay if we make it belong to us."

Joey looked at the broken chunks of wood from which the tree house was made. Most of it was old and rotted. "It looks kind of junky," he commented.

"We'll fix it up," said Dennis.

"I'll be the decorator!" announced Margaret excitedly. "We'll add on a special room for the babies and a powder room for when we have company."

Dennis and Joey rolled their eyes up and groaned.

"Forts don't have powder rooms," Dennis told Margaret.

"Oh, really?" replied Margaret. "Then where do the soldiers' wives go to freshen up?"

"Soldiers don't have wives, stupid!" exclaimed Joey.

"Don't call me stupid you baby-bottom kisser!" Margaret shouted back.

Joey turned red with embarrassment. The last thing he wanted was for Dennis to find out Margaret had tricked him earlier in her back yard.

Margaret looked eagerly at the old tree house. A plan was forming in her head. "It won't be a fort," she announced blinking her eyelashes at Dennis. "It'll be a house. A love nest!"

Once again, Dennis and Joey could only roll their eyes at each other and groan.

5.
Dennis Says
His Prayers

That evening at home Dennis finished everything off his dinner plate. Then he went outside to play with some of his friends. In the meantime his father washed the dishes and his mother balanced the family checkbook.

"How did Dennis do at the Wades'?" asked Henry as he scrubbed a plate.

"I guess the kids got along fine," replied Alice. "Penny said they weren't any trouble. She hardly saw them all day."

Henry could tell that Alice was still a little nervous about her new job with the real estate company. He stopped washing the dishes and sat down beside her.

"You feel good about work?" he asked her.

"I guess so," said Alice thinking about her first day on the job. "It was confusing. I tried to send a fax on the copy machine. The Federal Express man underestimated my age by five years."

"Congratulations!" exclaimed Henry.

"The bad news is," continued Alice, "I'm probably going to have to do some traveling. And soon. They want me to see their projects in Missouri, Oklahoma, and Nebraska. I would feel very strange leaving Dennis overnight."

"I gotta do it for *my* job," said Henry. "You get used to it."

"That's what I worry about," said Alice. "I don't want to get used to being away from Dennis. My mother was always home for me when I was a little girl."

"That didn't make her a better mother," said Henry in a reassuring tone of voice. "A child understands parents' motivation. He'll know in his heart you're doing it because you have to. If that wasn't the case, there wouldn't be any men who liked their fathers."

"Things are changing," Alice sighed.

"Not everything," Henry said warmly. "There are a few things that will always be the same."

Alice looked at Henry. His eyes were warm and loving. She felt lucky to be married to such a supportive man. She loved him very much.

The Wilsons always sat out on their front porch after their dinner. Mr. Wilson would sit in his rocking chair and smoke his pipe, while Martha would watch the neighborhood children who always came out to play in the evening.

From where they sat, the Wilsons could see that

28

the children were playing a game of hide-and-seek tonight. Dennis was "it" and had his face buried in a tree trunk where he was counting to twenty, while the other children scrambled to look for hiding places.

Tonight Mr. Wilson was in one of his grumpy moods, which wasn't unusual for him at all. When two little girls ran into his front lane in search of a hiding place he shooed them away with his pipe.

"This isn't a playground, girls," he said to them. "Throw it in reverse."

The girls quickly ran away from Mr. Wilson. Martha felt badly for the little girls and threw her husband a look of disapproval.

"I was unbeatable in hide-and-seek," said Mr. Wilson remembering back to the time when he was a little boy.

"Hiding or seeking?" asked Martha.

"Both," replied Mr. Wilson. "I had a nose for hiding places."

"I wouldn't think you'd be good at hiding," commented Martha.

"Why not?"

"Weren't you fat?"

"I was husky," insisted Mr. Wilson.

Just then Mr. Wilson noticed that Gunther Bechman, a three-year-old, was watching where the other children were hiding. When Dennis turned around, Gunther pointed excitedly at a car in the driveway across the street.

"I see Joey and Mike!" shouted Dennis.

Just then Joey and Mike popped out from behind the car and tried to beat Dennis back to the counting tree before they got tagged.

Mr. Wilson jumped out of his rocking chair. "He's cheating!" he yelled.

"Let the children play, George," said Martha. It didn't bother her that Dennis was cheating. After all, it was all in play.

But Mr. Wilson took things a little more seriously. "Dennis is cheating," he said. "He's using the Bechman kid as a spy!"

Mr. Wilson set his pipe down and climbed down off the porch.

"What are you doing?" Martha called out to him.

"I'm going to even things up," he shouted back as he stormed across the lawn toward Gunther, who was now pointing at some bushes where some other children were hiding.

"Gunther!" Mr. Wilson called out in a pleasant-sounding voice. "Your dad's going to the ice-cream store. He wants to take you with him. Hurry up and get home!"

The words "ice cream" brought a big smile to Gunther's face. He ran off toward his own house.

Mr. Wilson was also smiling as he returned to his pipe and rocking chair. "It's fair now," he told Martha.

"You lied to a toddler, George," said Martha shaking her head in disapproval. "Think how dis-

30

appointed he's going to be when he gets home."

"Disappointment's going to be a big part of that kid's life," replied Mr. Wilson with certainty. "He's a foot too short for his age and he's got a crooked eye."

And with that Mr. Wilson picked up his pipe, relit it, and took a deep, satisfying puff.

Later that night, Dennis lay in bed saying his prayers. Alice sat next to him while Henry stood in the doorway and watched.

"God bless everybody," said Dennis. "In alphabetical order."

Alice crinkled her brow at Dennis. "It's very nice that you want to bless everybody," she told him. "But you should single out the people who are most important to you."

Dennis glanced up at Heaven. "Hold on a minute," he said. "My mom's telling me something. I'll be right back." Then he looked at his mother. "That takes a long time, Mom," he replied. "And it's very easy to leave someone out."

"If you forget someone, He'll understand," explained Alice. Then she kissed him. "Good night, sweetheart," she said.

"Good night, buddy," said Henry.

"Good night, old geezer," replied Dennis to his father.

"That's not a very nice way to say good night to your father," remarked Alice.

Dennis was a little confused. "If a kid's nickname is 'buddy', what's a dad's?" he asked.

" 'Dad'," said Alice.

"Good night, Dad," Dennis said to Henry. Henry smiled. Alice walked to the door. She turned one last time toward Dennis.

"Prayers," Alice reminded him. Then she and Henry left Dennis alone in his room.

When they were gone Dennis looked back up to Heaven.

"I'm back," he began. He thought for a minute about who he should single out for prayers and then continued. "Do everybody, but start with my mother, father, Ruff, who's my dog which you probably don't cover, but if you see the dog-god, pass it on. Grandma and Grandpa and Grandma and Grandpa. Joey, Mrs. Wilson, and Mr. Wilson. When you bless Mr. Wilson, be careful. He gets cranky when you try to help him. Thank you. Over and out."

And with that, Dennis slid further beneath his blankets and fell into a deep, peaceful sleep.

6.
Enter Switchblade Sam

Switchblade Sam was asleep in the empty car of a freight train when he was awakened by the sound of church bells ringing. The freight train was still moving through town when he woke up. He had hopped the train a few towns back and planned to go on until the end of the line, but something about those church bells was getting under his skin.

Any town with a church deserves to be robbed, he thought as he rose to his feet.

Switchblade Sam was tall and thin and had a patch over one eye. Some of his teeth were missing and the ones he had left were either rotted or yellow. He had a stubbly beard since he shaved only once or twice a week and there were several mean-looking scars across his cheeks from the many knife fights he had won over the years.

That's why they called him *Switchblade* Sam.

When he had risen to his feet and caught his balance, he moved to the side doors of the freight car and pulled them open just far enough so he could see what was outside.

The town whizzed by him. It was a green and gentle-looking suburban valley separated from the big city on the horizon by belts of farmland and some small factories. There were many two-story houses with cars in their driveways and picnic tables in their back yards. Over the low roofs of the houses and their shade trees, the church spire could be seen.

A greedy smile came over Switchblade Sam's face. He grabbed his grease-covered crumpled overcoat and slipped it over his dirty plaid shirt and baggy pants. Then he picked up his duffel bag and slipped it over his shoulder.

He looked out from the freight car and searched the ground as it sped by. He was looking for a good place to jump. Suddenly he saw a fairly soft-looking grassy knoll just ahead. As the train approached it, Switchblade Sam leaped out of the freight car and rolled down the hill.

A minute later he rose to his feet. His duffel bag was still on his shoulder. He had used it to cushion himself in the fall.

From where he stood Switchblade Sam had an overview of the entire town. He smiled to himself as he looked around.

"Ain't that a pretty sight," he laughed. He was already thinking of all the things he could steal and of all the trouble he could cause.

Switchblade Sam felt something stuck between his front teeth. He figured it was some of the food he had eaten before he hopped the freight train, food he had stolen from another town.

He pulled his switchblade knife from his pocket and snapped it open. It made a loud clicking noise as it straightened out. The knife was sharp and clean. In fact, it was the only clean thing on Switchblade Sam's entire body.

He raised the sharp tip of the knife to his mouth and began to work it between his yellowed front teeth until he dislodged the piece of food that was trapped there.

Then he looked at the town below and grinned. The church bells were ringing again.

7.
The Differences Between Men and Women

The next day Dennis, Joey, and Margaret loaded up a toy stroller with tools and headed toward Turley's Woods. While Joey pushed the stroller, Dennis carried some extra pieces of lumber in his arms. Margaret marched alongside them carrying a small piece of plush carpeting.

Most of the tools they were bringing were important for building a fort. There was a hammer, a box of nails, some glue, and rolls of tape.

But some of the things in the stroller were not as important. Like Margaret's doll that sat on top of the box of nails. It looked like a kid going for a ride in a supermarket shopping cart. In fact, Dennis did not like the idea of carrying the supplies in Margaret's stroller at all. He would have preferred his own junk-finding wagon.

But Margaret insisted that they use the stroller, with that special way of getting what she wanted. Like threatening to tell Dennis's mother that he and Joey had forced her to sneak off to the woods yesterday when they were supposed to be playing in her back yard.

Margaret seemed to want to take charge of the whole project, which was typical of her. Even now she was practically leading the way. And she insisted that the piece of carpeting she was bringing along would look beautiful on the floor of the tree house. Dennis didn't think a fort was supposed to have carpeting. And he certainly did not think a fort was supposed to be "beautiful."

But then again, Margaret did not think they were going to build a fort at all. She thought they were going to build a home.

"We could have carried a lot more stuff if you didn't have to bring that idiotic doll and all her junk," Joey said to Margaret.

"She's not idiotic," said Margaret. "She's an important training tool. You know why men are so lousy when it comes to taking care of babies?"

Dennis smirked. "They have better things to do," he said snidely.

"Like what?" asked Margaret. "Play golf?"

"Hunting," answered Dennis. He was thinking of all the things he wanted to do when he grew up. Then he added: "Having wars. Driving cars. Shaving. Cleaning fish. Do you know how to do that?"

"I don't cut any animals open no matter how

cold and dumb they are," replied Margaret.

"If you didn't have men you wouldn't have fish," said Dennis.

"If you didn't have women, you wouldn't have babies, which means you wouldn't have people," replied Margaret. She felt satisfied she had outsmarted Dennis.

"You need men to have babies," Joey reminded her.

"Oh, really?" Margaret said defiantly. "How do you figure? Men don't have babies."

But Joey was ready with the right answer. "If you didn't have men," he said knowingly, "who would drive the ladies to the hospital?"

"Good one, Joey!" laughed Dennis. Then the two boys slapped their palms together in a high five.

Margaret was not going to be outdone by two dumb boys. Besides, she knew how ladies would get to the hospital without men. "They would take cabs," she said.

By the time the three children reached the tree house they were still discussing some of the important differences between men and women.

"There's other stuff that men do," said Joey as he brought the stroller to a full stop.

"With having babies?" asked Margaret. "Like what?"

"They call the relatives and tell them what happened."

"Big deal."

"The most important thing," Dennis said, "is that they marry the women. Then the women can go down and get the baby." Dennis knew that babies are waiting at the hospital for the women to pick them up after they get driven there by the men.

Margaret thought that was stupid. "The baby is in her stomach," she told Dennis.

"She has to get it installed," answered Dennis. "Her stomach isn't just filled up with babies."

Margaret did not believe that. "Who installs them?" she asked.

"A minister and a doctor," said Dennis with a ready answer. He hoped he was right.

"How?" asked Margaret, challenging him.

"How?" replied Dennis.

"Tell me, Dennis," Margaret challenged again.

"The belly button," said Dennis. "It opens up."

Margaret had a disbelieving look on her face.

"Not kids' belly buttons," continued Dennis. "After a woman gets married, it starts to open up."

"That's not true," insisted Margaret.

"Yep," said Joey. He agreed with Dennis.

"But how come men have belly buttons if they don't have babies?" Margaret asked smartly.

Easy, thought Dennis. "So they don't look weird in bathing suits," he said.

"You made that all up," said Margaret.

"It's true," Dennis insisted. "I heard it from a guy in the second grade."

Margaret squinted her eyes, suspicious. "You swear?" she asked.

"Cross my heart," said Dennis.

"What happens if you're swimming and your belly button opens?" asked Margaret.

"I guess you sink," answered Dennis. "That's why moms never go in the water."

Margaret had to admit to herself that Dennis's answers made good sense. Maybe that's why she liked him so much, she thought. He was pretty smart for a boy. She only wished he would act like he *liked* her a little more.

Well, maybe in time he would come around, she thought. . . .

In the meantime, Margaret tried her best to help Dennis and Joey rebuild the tree house. The three of them unloaded the stroller and carried the supplies up the rickety ladder and inside the house.

Margaret sawed some wood.

Dennis and Joey did some hammering.

But while they worked they didn't see the grimy visitor that had sneaked into the woods below. Switchblade Sam had heard the sound of the hammering and sawing and followed his ears to the tree house. Once there, he stepped carefully toward the toy stroller making sure the children couldn't see him. He had his switchblade in his hand.

He placed the tip of his switchblade gently under the sleeve of Margaret's doll, Baby Louise. Then he lifted the doll, stuffed it into his duffel bag, and ran away.

Switchblade Sam did not really need Margaret's doll. He did not even want it. He just thought that stealing it from a kid was a mean thing to do.

And Switchblade Sam *liked* doing mean things.

8.
Alice's New Job

Alice Mitchell sat around the conference table with the staff of the real estate company where she worked. Everyone was paying attention to the President of the company as he stood at the end of the table and pointed to the plans for a shopping mall that were pinned on a bulletin board.

Alice was still uncertain of herself around all these professional real estate brokers. There was so much to learn and she wanted to make a good impression.

The President had called the staff together to ask their advice on the shopping mall. He wanted to know why they weren't able to rent store space on the top floor. Alice had an idea why, so she raised her hand.

"Mitchell?" said the President, calling on her.

Alice hesitated. Should she tell her idea? she wondered.

"You have a toy store on the first floor," she reminded the President.

"Correct," he replied.

"You have a lot of traffic on the first floor because the big department stores are there," said Alice. "There's interest in the second level because that's where the restaurants are. We need something to draw traffic to the third level. Right?"

"Is there an echo in here?" said a woman from across the table. It was Andrea, another one of the brokers. From the first day Alice started with the company, she'd felt that Andrea didn't like her.

"Excuse me?" said Alice.

"We all know this," said Andrea regarding Alice's comments. She made Alice feel dumb.

"I'm sorry," said Alice. "I was just setting up what I was going to say. It's about the toy store on the first level. I know that you all know that there is a toy store on the first level. My suggestion is that you give the toy store six months free rent to move up to the top level."

There was a silence. Alice felt everyone was looking at her as if she had lost her mind.

"When I go to the mall with my little boy," she explained, "I can't get out unless we stop at the toy store. He knows he's not going to get anything unless it's a special occasion, but like every kid he wants to go in and look around."

"Spare us the family anecdotes, please," said Andrea snidely.

"Do you have children?" Alice asked Andrea.

"No," replied Andrea. "Can we go on? She's not making any sense."

"I'm not finished," said Alice, asserting herself.

Andrea laughed. "Last week you were making peanut butter sandwiches and wiping runny noses. Now you think you know how to sell retail space."

Alice continued despite Andrea's remarks. "There's always a lot of traffic in toy stores. If people go up to the third level to visit the toy store, they'll go through the other levels to get there. That's apparent to anyone with kids and you have to assume, maybe, that potential tenants might have kids and would know that, and it might entice them to take space on the upper levels. That's all I'm saying."

There was another silence in the room. Alice felt even dumber. But then the President nodded his head and smiled.

"Interesting point," he said. "Let's go on."

Alice relaxed. Maybe she could learn this job after all, she thought.

9.
Mrs. Wade Gets a Surprise

Two hours later the children stood at the foot of the tree and looked proudly up at their handiwork. They had repaired the tree house. Holes in the roof and walls had been patched with new pieces of wood. The floors and windowsills had been dusted and washed.

"We did a pretty good job," said Dennis proudly. "Rain won't get in now even if it rains sideways or upside down."

"How about a little paint?" suggested Joey.

"Couldn't hurt," agreed Dennis.

"You got any?"

"My dad does."

No sooner had the boys decided on their next task than Joey felt a sharp pain on the side of his head. Margaret had grabbed his ear lobe and was twisting it as hard as she could. She had just returned from her stroller where she discovered Baby Louise was missing.

"Gimme my doll, you jerk!" yelled Margaret.

"I don't have it!" Joey screamed.

Margaret turned to Dennis. "Give it to me, Dennis," she said.

"I didn't take your doll," said Dennis.

"It's not here!" exclaimed Margaret. "Somebody took it!"

"Not us," said Joey. "We've been with you."

"You guys swear you didn't take it?" asked Margaret.

"Yup." Dennis and Joey crossed their hearts and nodded their heads.

Margaret glanced back at her empty stroller. "I've been robbed!" she gasped.

On the way home Dennis and Joey picked up a lot of good junk for the tree house. They found an old lamp, some curtains, and a watering can with a bent spout.

Margaret was not interested in looking for junk. All she could think about was what happened to Baby Louise. She had received the doll from her great-grandmother and was supposed to give it to her own daughter when she grew up.

Now Baby Louise was gone. And how would she tell her mother without giving away that she and the boys had been playing in the woods — a place where they were not allowed to play without a parent present.

"Tell your mom that she fell in the sewer and got washed away into the ocean," was Dennis's suggestion to explain the disappearance of Baby Louise.

"I can't lie to my mother," said Margaret.

"Yep," agreed Joey. "They always know when you're doing it."

But Dennis had a plan. "*You* don't have to lie to her," he told Margaret. "Me and Joey will."

When Dennis and Joey reached Margaret's house, the first thing they did was look for Mrs. Wade. They looked in the kitchen and in the back yard and in the basement where the washer and dryer were. Still, they could not find her.

Then they went upstairs to look in the bedrooms. They went into Mrs. Wade's bedroom and heard the shower running in the bathroom. They went inside the bathroom and saw that Margaret's mother was hidden behind the shower curtain taking a shower. They knew it was not polite to interrupt someone when they were in the middle of a shower so they stood outside the bathtub and waited as patiently as they could.

Mrs. Wade did not know that anybody was standing in the bathroom waiting for her. When she finished washing she turned off the running water and slid open the shower curtain.

She was shocked to see the two little boys looking up at her.

"Guess what happened to Margaret's doll!" shouted Dennis.

Mrs. Wade screamed in embarrassment and quickly closed the shower curtain.

Dennis and Joey looked at each other. They were puzzled.

"Maybe she gots her belly button exposed!" said Joey.

Dennis nodded in agreement.

10.
An Apple a Day Won't Keep the Burglar Away

Switchblade Sam had spent most of his day getting a good look at the town. He wandered anywhere and everywhere. In the parks, around the factories, even around the school yard. Everywhere he went he saw the opportunity to be mean and nasty.

The main thing Switchblade Sam was looking for was something to steal. Something valuable that would bring him money. He knew if he looked around long enough he would find it.

He continued to walk through town until he came upon a neighborhood with many houses. He noticed that all the houses were very neatly kept, with nicely trimmed gardens in their back yards.

In one of the back yards Switchblade Sam noticed Gunther sitting in a swing eating a jumbo apple. The apple looked sweet and tasty to Switchblade Sam, who had not eaten much since he jumped off the freight train.

Switchblade Sam sneaked closer to Gunther and

49

eyed the apple. A loud grumble came from his stomach.

Gunther looked up and saw Switchblade Sam. He was a frightening sight.

"Whatcha eatin' there, sport?" asked Switchblade Sam.

Gunther held up the apple. "A apple," he replied cautiously.

The next thing Gunther saw was the big pointy blade of Switchblade Sam's knife. Switchblade Sam had snapped it open right in front of Gunther's eyes. Then Switchblade Sam stabbed Gunther's apple, yanked it away from the boy, and took a big bite out of it.

Switchblade Sam liked the apple. It was sweet and juicy and filling. He smiled as he ate it, and winked at Gunther.

Then he ran off down the street.

Switchblade Sam took big, juicy bites of his apple as he strolled down the street. He headed into an alley. Each time he came to somebody's house he looked at their back yard to see if he could find any unlocked doors.

Just as he was about to take the last bite of his apple, he happened to notice some curtains fluttering through the open window of a house across the alleyway. He looked both ways to see if anybody was around and then crossed the alley.

He cautiously slinked his way across the back yard of the house and made his way to the open window. Inside he could see expensive furniture. Next to the window sat an antique jewelry box. It was just within arm's reach . . . and Switchblade Sam knew he had just the arms with which to reach it.

11.
"He's Only a Boy!"

That evening Dennis went into the garage to
look for the paint he needed to paint the tree
house. His father kept half-a-dozen used cans of
paint on a wooden shelf. Dennis opened each one.
One of the cans was empty. In another, the paint
had dried up. But when he opened yet another
one, a big glop of wet white house paint spilled
out and landed on the garage floor.

Oops.

At the same time Dennis was making a mess in
the garage, Alice and Henry were getting ready
to go out to a restaurant for dinner. It was their
first night out alone since Alice had started her
new job.

Just before 6:30 PM the doorbell rang. It was
Polly, a pretty teenage girl who the Mitchells had
hired to baby-sit Dennis for the evening. That
night Polly showed up at the Mitchells' complete
with a helmet and heavy-duty long pants. "My

girlfriend used to baby-sit for Dennis," she explained.

"Dennis! We're leaving!" called Alice a few minutes later as she and Henry emerged from the house. "Don't give Polly a hard time!"

Dennis poked his head out of the garage and waved good-bye to his parents. After watching them drive off he went back to what he was doing: trying to clean up the spilled paint from the garage floor with a vacuum cleaner that was twice his size. So far he was doing pretty well. Not only was he getting up a lot of the paint, but the vacuum cleaner hose was picking up a lot of old nails and wood chips as well.

Satisfied that he was getting the job done, Dennis rested the vacuum cleaner hose against his shoulder and felt around for the off-switch. The hose was facing upward toward the open door of the garage. When he found the switch he tried to flip it with his free hand, only it flipped too far and sent the vacuum motor into reverse.

All the debris from inside the vacuum cleaner, all the wood chips and nails that were now a big glob of paint, came shooting straight out of the top of the hose, into the sky . . .

. . . and right over the fence into the Wilsons' back yard.

Dennis raced to the fence and peeked through. He could see Mr. Wilson placing a couple of raw chickens on his barbecue grill. Then, when Mr. Wilson bent down to get the barbecue lid, Dennis saw the flying glob of debris fall from the sky and land right on both chickens. Mr. Wilson stood up and covered the grill with the lid. He had not seen a thing.

Dennis hoped Mr. Wilson liked the taste of paint. . . .

A little while later George and Martha Wilson sat down at their patio table chewing their chicken. It had a funny taste to it.

"Tastes like paint," said Mr. Wilson as he chewed. "And wood."

Martha put down her fork. She couldn't take another bite. "I'll make us some sandwiches," she said rising from the table.

George looked down at the chicken. He poked some of it with his fork. He wondered how the chicken could get that ruined.

Then he looked over the fence to the house next door. Dennis's house.

It was the only possible explanation. . . .

Later that night Dennis was sitting in the bathtub, practically buried under a mound of bubbles. Polly's boyfriend, Mickey, had come over and was reading Dennis's favorite bedtime story aloud.

" *'Do not cry, little locomotive,'* said old *Engine*

#99 to Huffy," read Mickey. " 'Someday when you grow up you will realize that all trains are important, even mail trains.' "

Mickey stopped reading. "Wait a minute," he said. "How can a train grow?"

"He eats all his coal and gets plenty of sleep," explained Dennis.

"Yeah, right," said Mickey. "What's the point of reading lies?"

"It teaches kids to eat all their food and go to bed when they're supposed to and not cry when mean cabooses and boxcars make fun of you," Dennis replied.

"This is stupid," said Mickey. "You ready to get outta there and go to bed?"

"I haven't played submarine," Dennis insisted. "I haven't knocked all my guys in the water and rescued them. I'm not even wrinkled up yet. Keep reading."

Mickey sighed and continued to read: *"Huffy grabbed the mail bag as he raced past the Tooterville depot. 'A letter for the president!' said Huffy. 'I have to deliver a letter to the president!' "*

"You skipped a whole bunch," said Dennis. "You went right to the end. Go back."

Mickey groaned and turned back to the middle of the story. " *'I will never be big enough to pull anything but silly old mail cars,' sobbed Huffy,*" he read.

* * *

Later that night Dennis lay in bed holding his teddy bear. He was wide awake. Now Dennis could hear Polly and Mickey in the living room.

They were *smooching*.

Dennis did not see the fun in smooching. And he was in the mood for some fun. He decided to play a trick on the teenagers.

First he snuck downstairs and past the darkened living room where Polly and Mickey were kissing. Then he quietly opened the front door and went outside.

Once outside, he rang the doorbell to his house and then crouched behind the bushes.

A few seconds later Polly appeared at the front door and looked outside. Naturally, she did not find anybody there.

Dennis watched her from the bushes. He kept his hand over his mouth so she would not hear him giggling. Finally, Polly went back inside the house.

At the same time Dennis was playing tricks on his baby-sitter, Mr. Wilson was sneaking into the Mitchells' back yard determined to find proof that Dennis had been responsible for ruining his dinner.

But as soon as he crossed into the Mitchells' back yard he accidentally stepped in Dennis's small inflatable swimming pool. Now his foot was soaking wet.

He hopped around on one leg and tried to shake the water off his foot. Soon all that hopping moved him further across the yard until his leg landed on Dennis's bike horn, which was lying on the ground.

HONK! The bike horn was so loud that it woke Ruff up from his deep doggie sleep in the kitchen. It was Ruff's job to investigate any strange noises in the back yard. So he barked and ran out his doggie door in search of an intruder.

When Mr. Wilson saw Ruff bolt toward him, he quickly turned and ran back toward his own yard. But Ruff was catching up with him fast. Mr. Wilson ran toward a tree in the Mitchells' back yard. A rubber-tire swing was hanging from a branch of the tree by a piece of rope. Mr. Wilson grabbed onto the tire swing and pulled himself off the ground.

But Mr. Wilson was so heavy that the tire swing not only swayed forward, but the branch that it was tied to suddenly snapped!

Mr. Wilson came falling down, the tire in his arms, and landed flat on his back in Dennis's sandbox. Before he could get up, Ruff was standing over him.

"Get away!" Mr. Wilson commanded in a whisper. "Go on! Shoo!"

But then Ruff recognized Mr. Wilson and was happy to see him. So happy that he nuzzled Mr.

Wilson with his wet nose and licked him with his big floppy tongue. . . .

Polly and Mickey had just begun kissing again when the doorbell rang a second time. This time they were fed up. They realized that some neighborhood kid was probably playing a practical joke on them.

They decided to get even.

Mickey went down into the Mitchells' basement and found a box of carpet tacks. Upstairs, Polly filled a mop bucket with water from the bathtub. Then she squirted a hefty amount of bath bubbles into it.

Outside, Dennis continued to ring the doorbell. He wondered why it was taking the teenagers so long to answer the door. . . .

Mr. Wilson had gotten out of the sandbox and was now limping across the Mitchells' back yard to their garage. He could see the spilled paint all over the garage floor. Then he noticed the smell of paint coming from the spout of the vacuum cleaner hose.

It did not take Mr. Wilson long to realize how Dennis had ruined his barbecue dinner. Somehow Dennis must have filled the hose with painted debris, and shot it into his barbecue grill when his back was turned. Now he had the evidence he

needed to prove what kind of menace that kid really was.

But first he had to make sure his theory was right. He threw the hose on the ground, bent over the vacuum cleaner, and flicked the "on" switch. He did not notice that the hose had landed right next to an old, scuffed golf ball that was lying on the floor.

The vacuum hose sucked the golf ball into its nozzle, blocking the hose. The force of the suction inside the vacuum cleaner made the hose move wildly on its own until it rose up between Mr. Wilson's legs.

Mr. Wilson tried to get control of the wiry hose, but he looked more like a rodeo rider being thrown up and down on a wild bronco.

Finally, Mr. Wilson was able to reach over and throw the "on" switch into reverse. As soon as he did, the golf ball shot out of the vacuum hose and hit him right between the eyes!

Mr. Wilson screamed in agony. . . .

Dennis was watching from the bushes as Mickey took a look out the front door. Mickey looked both ways.

"I guess those kids took off!" he heard Mickey call to Polly inside. Then Mickey went back inside and turned the house lights off.

Dennis was disappointed. He thought that Polly

and Mickey would try to trick whoever it was they thought was ringing the bell, but it sounded as if they had just given up.

Dennis decided to try the bell trick one more time. He climbed out from behind the bushes and started up toward the porch when, suddenly, he saw a hunched figure come limping from behind the house. The figure was groaning in pain.

The figure frightened Dennis. It was too dark for him to see that it was only Mr. Wilson.

Dennis ran around to the other side of the house, into the kitchen, and locked the door behind him.

Mr. Wilson, on the other hand, was raging mad.

"I got him this time," he grumbled to himself as he limped his way to the front door. "Mitchell can't deny it!"

And he pressed his fingers into the doorbell. But tonight the doorbell felt a little funny. A sharp pain shot through Mr. Wilson's thumb. He looked down. Somebody had taped a thumbtack to the doorbell!

Mr. Wilson threw his head back and screamed in pain.

He pulled his thumb off the tack and put it in his mouth to soothe the pain. That was when he heard the front door open. He looked up to see a cloud of flour being hurled right into his face! He could not see that it was Mickey who threw the flour so he thought it must have been Dennis!

Mickey shut the front door so quickly he did not see that he had just doused Mr. Wilson — not some prank-playing neighborhood kids!

And as Mr. Wilson coughed puffs of flour out from under his moustache he suddenly heard the window to the upstairs bathroom slide open. No sooner did he look up through white-caked eyelids, than he saw a gallon of sudsy water spilling down at him! *Splash!* Mr. Wilson was drenched.

He never saw that it was Polly who spilled the water on him. He never knew that the teenagers thought he was somebody else.

He could only think that it must have been Dennis who was out to get him. Dennis who put a thumbtack on the doorbell. Dennis who doused him with flour. Dennis who spilled sudsy water on him.

"He's only a boy," Martha had said to him the other day.

Mr. Wilson thought of those words now and groaned.

12.
A Dennis Mitchell Apology

Dennis arrived at Mr. Wilson's back door bright and early the next morning. He had gotten up before everybody else, even before his mother came downstairs to make breakfast, so he could apologize to Mr. Wilson.

"Hi, Mrs. Wilson," said Dennis. Through the back screen door he could see Martha in the kitchen, making breakfast. "Is Mr. Wilson up?"

"Not yet, dear," Martha said as she opened the door to let him inside.

"How long do you think he's gonna sleep for?" asked Dennis.

"Not much longer," answered Martha. "He's having his picture taken this morning."

"For what?"

"For the newspaper."

"Did he get arrested?"

Martha smiled. "He's being honored for his garden," she said.

"Do you think he'd get mad if I went upstairs?"

"If you disturbed him he might," said Martha. "What do you want to go upstairs for?"

Dennis held up a folded piece of colored craft paper. "I made him an 'I'm Sorry Ruff Chewed Up Your Shoe That You Had Since The Good Old Days' card."

"That's very nice, Dennis," Martha said, smiling at the little boy's thoughtfulness. "I'm sure Mr. Wilson will appreciate it."

"I'm kind of busy today so I won't have a chance to give it to him," said Dennis. "I have to go to Margaret's house because we're getting poor and my mom has a job now. Could I just put it by his whisker cutter so he'll see it as soon as he gets up? That's where I put all my dad's sorry cards.

"It's a good time to say you're sorry because grown-up guys are happy when they wake up," Dennis continued. "My dad's so happy in the morning, he whistles when he goes to the bathroom — "

But Martha did not have the time to listen to Dennis anymore. She had to finish making the breakfast. "You can go up if you promise not to disturb Mr. Wilson," she told him.

"I promise!" said Dennis. He headed for the living room, then stopped and turned back. "You know what?" he called out to Martha. "You're the nicest ol' gal on the block!"

Then he scooted up the stairs.

* * *

Mr. Wilson lay in his bed, snoring loudly, as Dennis tiptoed past him and into the bathroom.

Dennis was careful not to wake Mr. Wilson. He quietly placed his sorry card right up against Mr. Wilson's shaving brush and then quickly turned to leave.

But as he turned he caught sight of something too funny to ignore. It was Mr. Wilson's teeth — his *dentures* — soaking in a glass on the bathroom sink.

Dennis quickly listened for the sound of Mr. Wilson's snoring. Good. Mr. Wilson was still fast asleep.

Dennis carefully lifted the dentures out of the glass and examined them. He held them up to his own mouth. The teeth of the dentures were kind of big.

"Hello, I'm Dennis," he said laughing. "These are my new teeth. I'm the doctor. Open your mouth and say 'aah'!"

Dennis opened his mouth as wide as he could and wiggled his tongue out through the dentures just the way he would at the doctor's.

Suddenly Dennis felt like a wild jungle tiger with ferocious sharp teeth and jaws. He opened his mouth even wider and growled. Then he clamped the teeth together mightily.

But when the denture plates smashed together the two front teeth broke off, bounced into the sink, and tumbled down the drain.

They were gone.

And Mr. Wilson's dentures were broken.

Oops.

Dennis ran back to his house and up into his room. He had to think of some way to repair the fake choppers before Mr. Wilson woke up.

He reached under his bed and pulled out his toy box. Inside the toy box was a treasure chest. Inside the treasure chest was a toy bank with a lock on it. The bank was Dennis's special hiding place. Inside were all the things he kept for special emergencies. And this was a super-special emergency!

Dennis dialed the combination on the lock until the bank's door popped open. Then he began looking for something, *anything*, that could replace the two front teeth on Mr. Wilson's dentures.

He found a Milky Way bar. No, he thought. Too gooey.

Then he pulled out an old watch. No, he thought. Too loud.

He found two dirty copper pennies. The right size, he thought, but the wrong color!

Finally Dennis found exactly what he was looking for: an old mini-pack of Chiclets gum. They were the perfect size and color for front teeth. Not only that, they were so old that they had become stale. Now they were as hard as real teeth!

* * *

"George? Are you ready?" called Martha from the living room. "The photographer is here!"

Mr. Wilson was awakened by Martha's call. He had overslept. He leaped out of bed, splashed some water on his face, shaved, and quickly got dressed in his best suit. By the time he appeared on the back patio he was still fiddling with his dentures trying to get them to fit in his mouth just right.

They felt a little funny this morning. . . .

Martha and the photographer were waiting in Mr. Wilson's garden. The photographer was getting a little impatient. He had several other places to go that morning.

As soon as Mr. Wilson stood in front of his garden the photographer looked through the lens of his camera. Now he was ready to take Mr. Wilson's picture.

"That's good," the photographer called out to Mr. Wilson. "Gimme a smile!"

Martha watched proudly as her husband posed in front of his garden and smiled. But as soon as Mr. Wilson opened his lips Martha gasped in alarm.

Mr. Wilson's two front teeth were suddenly bigger and more crooked than usual. It now looked like Mr. Wilson had a huge overbite. He looked positively goofy!

In fact, when Martha squinted her eyes to get a better look, she realized that those were not Mr.

Wilson's front teeth at all. They were two pieces of chewing gum!

But by then it was too late.

FLASH! The photographer took the picture.

Now the whole town would see Mr. Wilson and his grotesque smile in the morning newspaper.

13.
Switchblade Sam Gets Some Advice

In another part of town, Switchblade Sam was getting restless. He had already stolen a little girl's doll and he had snatched an apple away from a little boy.

But those were small pickings compared to what he really wanted: money.

As he sat in the park, he lit a cigarette and looked around for anyone that he might be able to steal some money from. Then he saw a group of teenage girls who were tending to a collection of babies and toddlers on the park lawn.

Baby-sitters! realized Switchblade Sam. And baby-sitters made money. In fact, Switchblade Sam could see a purse dangling over the handle of one of the strollers.

Switchblade Sam grinned when he saw the purse. He threw his cigarette to the ground and rose to his feet. In a matter of minutes, he knew, that purse would be his.

Folding his overcoat over his arm he moved

slowly toward the group of girls and toddlers. He inched his way toward the stroller with the dangling purse, but came to a sudden stop when he realized he was being watched by one of the toddlers.

It was Gunther!

Switchblade Sam smiled at Gunther, but Gunther was frightened of the mean-looking apple stealer. He just continued to stare at him with his big wide eyes.

Just then a police car pulled up at the edge of the park. Inside was the Police Chief. He had been cruising the neighborhood making sure all was well, when he saw Switchblade Sam hanging around the park. He did not recognize Switchblade Sam and thought he had better investigate.

When Switchblade Sam saw the Police Chief crossing the park toward him, he motioned for Gunther to keep quiet. But Gunther was so frightened he just turned and ran off to join the other toddlers.

Switchblade Sam watched as the Police Chief approached. He had to be careful not to look as mean and ugly as he usually did, which for Switchblade Sam was no small trick.

"I don't believe I've seen you around here," said the Police Chief in a suspicious tone.

"Maybe that's 'cause I ain't never been around here," Switchblade Sam cautiously answered.

The Police Chief squinted his eyes at Switchblade Sam. This was the meanest-looking stranger he had ever seen. "What're you up to?" he asked in an even more suspicious tone of voice.

"What's it to ya'?" answered Switchblade Sam.

The Police Chief took one look at Switchblade Sam and knew he was trouble. He decided to give him a warning.

"I run a real nice, clean town," he said. "I don't want any trouble. My advice to you is, follow the sun outta here."

Switchblade Sam spit an apple seed from his mouth. He did not like being bullied by a policeman, especially when he had not done anything wrong yet! He knew his rights as a citizen. He decided to tell the Police Chief so.

"Times have changed, officer," said Switchblade Sam. "I ain't somebody you can run outta town on a rail. I ain't no bum. I'm an oppressed man. You mess with me, you better have a good, lawful reason."

"We have a vagrancy ordinance," said the Police Chief.

Switchblade Sam did not want to make the Police Chief angry. He needed time to make good on his plan to find something in town to steal.

"The only reason I ain't moving on is you stopped me to give me the breeze," he said. "Take a good look at my face. You'll be a real lucky cop if you ever see it again."

Switchblade Sam gave the Police Chief a wide

70

smile that revealed all of his rotten teeth. The Police Chief backed off, disgusted at the sight. Then Switchblade Sam pushed past the Police Chief and walked away.

The Police Chief watched as Switchblade Sam disappeared down the street. He knew he would have to keep his eyes on that one.

But Switchblade Sam felt happy as he walked away from the park. He slipped his hand beneath his overcoat, which was still folded over one arm. The purse that had been dangling from the stroller was now dangling from his arm.

He managed to slip it there just before the Police Chief had reached him.

14.
Baby-sitter Dilemma

Henry Mitchell had to go out of town on a business trip.

That same day Alice Mitchell found out she had to go on a business trip as well.

Both she and her husband would be out of town at the same time.

It would be the first time Dennis would be completely alone.

To make matters worse, the Mitchells could not find an overnight baby-sitter. Since her last experience baby-sitting for Dennis, Polly swore never to work for the Mitchells again.

That was true for every baby-sitter in town. Word gets around.

The only person Alice had not asked to baby-sit Dennis was Martha Wilson. That was because Martha was married to Mr. Wilson. Alice knew it was not a good idea to force Dennis on Mr. Wilson, but she was desperate.

To Alice's surprise Martha was more than happy to have Dennis spend a night in her home. As long as Alice and Henry got back before Mr. Wilson's garden party that weekend, Dennis would be more than welcome.

The next morning Alice and Dennis appeared on the Wilsons' doorstep. Dennis's suitcase was packed full. Mr. Wilson emerged from inside the house.

"Hey, Mr. Wilson," said Dennis happily. "I'm sleeping at your joint!"

"So I hear," said Mr. Wilson in a disgruntled voice. He was not thrilled at the idea.

"I brought you some grasshoppers!"

"You shouldn't have," Mr. Wilson said with a groan.

Alice and Henry left Dennis with the Wilsons and then drove off to the airport for their trips. As they drove away, Alice started to cry. She did not like the idea of leaving Dennis even for one day.

Dennis and the Wilsons waved good-bye to the Mitchells from the Wilsons' front porch. Dennis was not as sad as his mother was about his being left alone.

"You know what, Mr. Wilson?" he said. "You know why I'm not crying? Because if I'm not going to be around my mom and dad, the only other person that I want to be with is you."

Martha smiled. She was touched at Dennis's sentiment. But Mr. Wilson could only groan.

"I can't tell you how deeply moved I am," he said grimly. Then he picked up Dennis's suitcase and opened the door to let the little menace inside his home.

15.
A Night at the Wilsons'

It was raining that evening. Mr. Wilson had settled in behind his desk in his den. Spread out before him was his coin collection. He wore special white gloves as he handled the ancient coins and looked at each one through a magnifying glass.

For Mr. Wilson, examining his coin collection was the most relaxing way to spend a rainy evening.

But for Dennis, who was sitting on the leather sofa not far from Mr. Wilson's desk, the evening was getting kind of boring. There was little for a five-year-old boy to do in the Wilsons' house. For the last few minutes he had been restlessly kicking his heels against the side of the sofa.

The last few kicks were starting to annoy Mr. Wilson.

"Don't do that," Mr. Wilson ordered.

"What?" asked Dennis innocently.

"Don't kick my couch."

Dennis realized what he was doing and stopped swinging his legs. "There sure isn't much to do here when it's raining outside," he said after a pause.

Mr. Wilson did not respond. He was too busy concentrating on his coin collection.

"Do you want to play cards?" Dennis asked.

"No," said Mr. Wilson.

"Do you want to go put your old Navy clothes on and play war?"

"No, I don't," Mr. Wilson insisted.

"How about — "

"I'm busy, Dennis," Mr. Wilson finally said.

"Can I help?" asked Dennis.

"No."

"How come?"

"Because you can't."

Dennis frowned. "That's not a very good answer," he said. Then he craned his neck to try to get a good look at Mr. Wilson's coin collection. "Is that pirate's gold?" he asked.

"No," said Mr. Wilson.

"Is it real valuable?" asked Dennis.

"Yes," said Mr. Wilson.

"How much money is all that worth?"

Mr. Wilson smiled. "More than you'll ever have," he said proudly.

"Is that why you keep it locked up in your safe?" asked Dennis.

"Uh-huh."

Dennis remembered seeing Mr. Wilson take his coin collection from a special safe in the bookcase. The safe had a special surface that looked like a row of books.

"How come that safe looks like books?" he asked.

Mr. Wilson sighed. "Why do you ask so many questions?"

"I've only been around for five years," explained Dennis. "There's a lot of stuff I don't know."

Mr. Wilson gave up. There was just no stopping it when Dennis became curious.

"The safe looks like books so that if a thief comes in, he won't recognize it," said Mr. Wilson.

"Is a thief a robber?" asked Dennis.

"Yeah."

"You ever have a robber here?"

"No."

"Then how come you got that safe?"

Mr. Wilson sighed again. He was getting exasperated. "I have it *in case* a robber comes," he explained.

Dennis did not quite understand. "If your safe looks like books, why would a robber come?" he asked.

"He wouldn't," answered Mr. Wilson. "That's the point."

Dennis thought for a second. Then he realized

something. Something Mr. Wilson probably never even thought of. "What if he was a *book* robber?" he asked.

"If he was a book robber," said Mr. Wilson, "he probably wouldn't be interested in my coins."

"You got everything figured out, don't you Mr. Wilson?" Dennis smiled.

Mr. Wilson tightened his lips. "I haven't figured out how to get my work done with you in the house," he said angrily.

Dennis nodded. "That's a tough one," he agreed.

When Dennis was wrinkled enough, he knew it was time to get out of Mr. Wilson's bathtub. He climbed out of the tub and dried himself off with one of Martha Wilson's fresh-smelling fluffy towels. Then, after wrapping himself in the towel, he brushed his teeth.

As he brushed he noticed a bottle of nasal spray on the glass shelf above the bathroom sink. He stopped brushing and took the spray bottle down from the shelf. He became fascinated with it and took the top off the bottle.

Then he squeezed it. The nasal fluid emptied out of the bottle like a fountain gushing water. Dennis liked the way that looked.

So he squeezed . . .

and squeezed . . .

and squeezed . . . until the bottle was completely empty.

Oops.

Now what could he do? If Mr. Wilson found his nasal spray bottle empty he would know who was responsible.

Dennis looked around the medicine chest for something to replace the nasal fluid. He found a bottle of mouthwash. It looked good enough. He began pouring the mouthwash into the nasal spray bottle. Most of the mouthwash fell over his hands and into the sink, but enough of it made it into the spray bottle.

However, when Dennis finished filling the spray bottle he saw he had a new problem: the mouthwash bottle was now empty.

Oops.

Again he needed a refill. He bent down under the sink and opened the vanity cabinet. He saw bottles and bottles of different kinds of household cleansers. One bottle was filled with a liquid that was the same color as the mouthwash. Dennis opened the bottle of cleanser and noticed that it had a fresh, pine-smelling scent.

Mr. Wilson would never know the difference.

Dennis filled the mouthwash bottle with the pine detergent. Then he returned the mouthwash bottle to the medicine chest, went down the hall to the guest bedroom, and put on his pajamas.

When he had climbed into the guest bed, Martha came in to say good night.

"How about if I recite my favorite poem when I was your age?" she asked Dennis.

"Is it about flowers and lambs?" asked Dennis. He wanted to make sure it wasn't a girl's poem.

"No," Martha gently answered.

"Okay," said Dennis. Dennis liked Martha Wilson just as much as he liked Mr. Wilson. Martha was different from her husband. She did not get mad at Dennis like Mr. Wilson did. Dennis knew that that was because the Wilsons never had any children of their own. He knew that Martha liked him because he reminded her of what it might be like if she did have her own kids. He also knew that that was why she had agreed to baby-sit him when everyone else in town refused.

Dennis listened patiently as Martha recited the bedtime poem. It was a baby's poem, and Dennis thought he was too old for it. But he did not say that to Martha. You don't tell someone you like that their bedtime poem is for babies. Especially when you know it makes that person feel good to recite it to you. Instead, Dennis pretended that he liked the poem so much that it made him drowsy enough to fall asleep.

When Martha finished the poem, and saw that Dennis's eyes were closed in sleep, she left the guest room.

As soon as she was gone Dennis opened his eyes.

That was when he heard the screams coming from Mr. Wilson's bathroom.

It was Mr. Wilson screaming.

Dennis wondered if Mr. Wilson might have noticed the different taste of the mouthwash.

16.
A Ruff Night

Mr. Wilson lay flat on his back in a sudsy puddle of water on his bathroom floor. Just one minute before, he had gone into the bathroom to wash up for bed. No sooner did his foot touch the wet tile floor, than he slipped and lost his balance. In a matter of seconds his feet were flying up over his head and he was hitting the floor with a *thud*.

That was the first scream Dennis heard from way down the hall in the guest room.

When Mr. Wilson picked himself up from the floor his pajamas were completely soaked.

Mr. Wilson decided to finish washing up before changing into dry pajamas. He opened the medicine cabinet and pulled down his bottle of mouthwash. A good swish and gargle was always just what he needed before bedtime.

He poured the mouthwash into his gargling glass and brought it to his lips. It had a cleaner-than-usual scent to it that night. *Must get stronger with age*, thought Mr. Wilson.

He opened his mouth and took a drink of the liquid.

Then his mouth exploded with a stinging pain. His tongue and throat began to burn. His eyes bulged almost out of their sockets. His stomach turned.

He spit and gagged the liquid back into the sink. It wasn't his mouthwash at all. It tasted more like household cleanser!

That was the second scream Dennis heard from way down in the guest room.

After he washed his mouth out with fresh, cold water Mr. Wilson found himself sniffling. All that coughing and spitting had made him congested.

He reached into the medicine chest again. A good shot of nasal spray would clear him right up.

He removed the top of the small spray bottle and, covering one nostril with a finger, placed the tip of the bottle inside the other nostril.

Mr. Wilson frowned. The liquid gushed up into his nose, but he didn't feel a thing. He soon became aware that that was because his nose had become momentarily numb! After that, he felt a sting so sharp, so painful, that it seemed to burn a hole right up and out the top of his head!

That was the third and final scream Dennis heard from the guest room down the hall. After that, Mr. Wilson plunged his head into a sinkful of water and remained in that position until his head was soothed from the inside to the out.

Dennis was wide awake. He lay in the guest bed with a reading lamp on, but he had nothing to read. He had looked all around the room, but he couldn't find even a single comic book. There weren't even any superheroes printed on his blanket for him to look at.

Suddenly Dennis heard his dog, Ruff, baying outside. He went to the window and peeked through the curtain at his house across the way. Ruff was all alone over there. Dennis did not like the idea of that. Ruff sounded lonely and miserable.

Mr. Wilson's face was still puffy and red by the time he climbed into his bed and turned out the lights. Martha had just come from cleaning the mess in the bathroom. She took off her robe and climbed in next to him.

"I've never loved this house as much as I did today and tonight," she said to Mr. Wilson who was still awake.

"Don't go gooey on me, Martha," said Mr. Wilson. "It's the same darn house we've had for forty-one years. The only thing that's changed is the water heater and the toilet seat."

"The house is different with a child in it," insisted Martha.

"Yeah," said Mr. Wilson sourly. He was thinking of the mouthwash, the nasal spray, and the slippery wet bathroom floor. "It's noisy and dangerous."

Dennis had climbed out of his bed, sneaked downstairs and out the Wilsons' back door. He hurried across the Wilsons' driveway and around the fence to the back yard of his own house. There he found Ruff tied by a leash to his dog house. Ruff was glad to see Dennis. He jumped up and down gleefully as Dennis released him from the leash.

Then the two of them ran back across the driveway to the Wilsons' house.

Martha Wilson was having trouble falling asleep. She stared up at the ceiling.

"I recited a poem for Dennis tonight that my mother used to recite to me," she said to Mr. Wilson. "I remembered every word. In some tiny measure, my mother would be proud. I passed something on."

Now Mr. Wilson was having trouble sleeping, too. He knew that having Dennis around was making Martha happy and sad at the same time. She was happy to be able to take care of a child, but sad that she and Mr. Wilson never had one of their own.

"It's ten o'clock, Martha," said Mr. Wilson.

"Don't start with the regrets now."

"I can't help it, George," said Martha.

"Jeez," sighed Mr. Wilson. "This is the sort of thing a gal moans about in her thirties."

"I did," answered Martha. "And in my forties, in my fifties . . ."

"You're saying that for forty-six years we've been married you've felt you're missing something?"

Martha smiled sadly. "I'm not complaining, George," she replied. "I'm only saying that I'm enjoying taking care of a child."

"You're going deeper than *that*," said Mr. Wilson.

"Maybe I am," said Martha cautiously. She knew Mr. Wilson did not like to talk about the mistakes of the past.

"You can't cry over spilled milk that's spoiled, dried up, turned to dust, and blown around the globe six times," said Mr. Wilson.

Martha paused. "I would have been a good mother," she said thoughtfully.

Mr. Wilson didn't like regretting his mistakes. "Yeah," he answered. "And I would have been a good fireman."

And with that, he turned on his side and tried to fall asleep.

But Martha was restless. She got out of bed and put her bathrobe back on.

"Where are you going?" asked Mr. Wilson.

"To make myself a cup of tea," replied Martha.

Mr. Wilson wondered why Martha was so upset. After all, it wasn't *his* fault they never had children. It wasn't *anybody's* fault. For some people not being able to have children is very natural. At least, that's what their doctor told them many years before.

"I didn't decree that we wouldn't have children, Martha," Mr. Wilson reminded his wife. "That was out of both our hands. Okay? I'm not the villain."

Martha made her way to the bedroom door. "This isn't about having children or not having children, George," she said sharply. "It's about my feeling something very good and not being able to tell you about it."

She left the room. George felt as if a cold wind had crossed his bed. Martha was trying to tell him something very meaningful and he acted like he didn't care. He knew that was wrong. After a few moments he put on his robe and went downstairs to apologize.

He was heading for the kitchen when he caught sight of his easy chair in the living room. The lights were out, but he could just make out the wisps of Martha's gray hair over the back of the chair.

"Martha?" he called gently. He walked up behind the easy chair and stood there.

"I didn't mean to hurt you," he continued, clearing his throat sorrowfully. "I'm not terribly good with feelings and emotions."

Mr. Wilson placed his hands on the back of the easy chair.

"There are a lot of subjects I'd just as soon not discuss, let alone bring up," he said. He reached over the back of the easy chair and began to stroke Martha's gray hair. Her hair felt a little coarse, like it was covered with a little too much hair spray.

"I would like to have a son or a daughter," he added with a deep sigh. "But I'm an old horse and there's no getting me to gallop. You couldn't fire the fatherly feelings in me because they're not there. But that doesn't mean my feelings for you have gone cold. That'll never happen."

Mr. Wilson continued to stroke Martha's hair. Then he began to massage her head. He knew how relaxed that made her feel when she was upset.

"You've got all the love I have," he said. "I didn't share it with anybody but you."

He decided to kiss Martha. "Remember this?" he said as he closed his eyes and leaned over the back of the easy chair. *"Je t'aime."*

Mr. Wilson puckered his lips and moved closer to plant a kiss on his wife.

That's when he heard Martha's voice. "George?" she asked.

Only her voice sounded like it was coming from behind him.

If that was so, wondered Mr. Wilson, then who was he about to plant a big kiss on?

He opened his eyes. He saw two droopy eyes, some furry eyebrows, and a big, black, wet, runny nose!

It was Ruff's nose!

Mr. Wilson leaped back in surprise. Martha was standing far behind him watching from the foyer.

Dennis's dog was sitting in the easy chair happily wagging his tail!

Martha smiled at Mr. Wilson. The old softy. Despite his gruff manner he always found some way to show Martha that he really cared about her.

17.
A Stranger in the Tree House

The following morning Dennis found Mr. Wilson rummaging through the dusty attic. He was looking for the garden lanterns that he would need for the flower show later that evening.

Dennis wanted to help Mr. Wilson.

He turned an electric switch, which turned on the overhead fan. *Click!*

A cloud of dust blew into Mr. Wilson's face!

"Turn that off!" yelled Mr. Wilson, wiping the dust from his eyes.

Dennis turned the switch off. The dust settled down.

Then Dennis picked up a small box that was sitting on an old trunk. Maybe the garden lanterns were in there, he figured.

He pushed open the lid on the box.

About a hundred mothballs spilled out and bounced across the floor.

Mr. Wilson was getting frustrated. He couldn't find the garden lanterns anywhere in the attic.

He turned and marched angrily toward the attic stairs.

And right onto the floor full of rolling mothballs.

Mr. Wilson's feet came flying out from under him. His arms swung wildly as he tried to catch his balance, but he landed flat on his back.

Oops.

Dennis looked at Mr. Wilson. "When I grow up," he said, "I hope I never have a five-year-old. They're nothing but a big headache!"

Dennis excused himself from helping Mr. Wilson anymore that morning. He had an appointment to play with Joey and Margaret.

Mr. Wilson was not disappointed. In fact, he was counting the minutes until Dennis's mother would arrive to take Dennis home and far away from that evening's garden party.

Dennis met Joey and Margaret at the tree house. The three children scrambled up the ladder. But as soon as they poked their heads through the floor, they were startled by a surprising sight.

A strange-looking man in a dirty overcoat and a patch over one eye was sitting in their tree house!

He seemed to have been waiting for the children to arrive.

"Welcome," Switchblade Sam said to them with a grin that revealed his rotted, yellow teeth. The children remained frozen halfway through the tree house floor.

"There is nothing to be afraid of," said the stranger. "Come on in. I have something for you."

Switchblade Sam reached behind his back and pulled out Baby Louise. Margaret shouted with delight. Then Switchblade Sam reached behind his back again and pulled out a handful of candy bars. Dennis and Joey felt their sweet tooths tingle.

It was not long before the children had joined Switchblade Sam in the tree house. Margaret was holding Baby Louise, and Dennis and Joey were licking melted chocolate off their fingers.

Switchblade Sam watched the children, his one exposed eyeball jerking back and forth between them as they ate. "I guess we can be friends, huh?" he asked.

The children nodded happily.

Switchblade Sam took a half-smoked cigarette butt from his coat pocket and lit it with a match. He felt confident the children trusted him. That was important, since he had to find out where he could find valuable things to steal.

"You all live in nice homes, huh?" he asked them.

The children nodded.

"Lots of very nice things in them?"

Again the children nodded.

"I don't have much," said Switchblade Sam. "Everything I own is in my pockets. But what I do have, I'll share with you. Like how I found the baby doll and gave it back to you. And how I give you candy. If, say, I had a nice television set, you could have that, too."

"Really?" asked Joey. They could use a new TV in his house.

"Help me out," said Switchblade Sam. "What are some of the things you kiddies have in your houses?"

"Dining room set," said Margaret, wiping melted chocolate off of Baby Louise's mouth.

"Those are nice," said Switchblade Sam. "But I'm thinking of something you can put in your pocket or in a bag. Something valuable. Worth a lot of money. Like jewelry."

"My mom's got a lot of jewelry," said Margaret. "My grandma has even more. Grandmas wear lots of jewelry to cover up the spots on their skin."

"How about gold coins?" asked Dennis. He was thinking of Mr. Wilson's coin collection. You could fit those into a pocket.

Switchblade Sam's eyes widened with interest. "Oh, that's nice," he said.

"Yep," said Dennis. "They're real valuable."

"Are these coins in a safe place?" asked Switchblade Sam.

"Yep," answered Dennis still smacking his lips from the chocolate candy. "But it doesn't look like a safe. It looks like books. If you go downstairs where all the books are, you don't know there's gold there."

"Ain't that smart," grinned Switchblade Sam.

It was just the right kind of treasure he was looking for. But now that he had found out about it, he had to make sure Dennis and his friends would not give him away.

"Your folks ever tell you that if you talk with a stranger you're supposed to tell them about it?" he asked.

"Yep," answered Margaret. Dennis and Joey nodded, too.

"You don't gotta tell them about me," Switchblade Sam told them.

"How come?" asked Dennis.

" 'Cause I ain't a stranger," answered Switchblade Sam. "I'm a friend."

"Good point," agreed Margaret.

"If you was to tell them about me," explained the eye-patched man, "they might not understand that we're friends and they wouldn't let you come back here no more."

"*Any*more!" Margaret corrected him.

"That's right," smiled Switchblade Sam. "So it's best you keep quiet about me."

"Okay," said Dennis. He was speaking for everybody.

Switchblade Sam smiled with satisfaction. All that was left now was for him to follow Dennis and find out which house had the gold coins. "You better get going now," he told the children. "It's getting late."

Dennis, Margaret, and Joey climbed out of the

tree house and rode off on their bicycles. A moment later Switchblade Sam followed after them. He followed them out of Turley's Woods, around sidewalks, and through the alleys of town. He watched as they split up and went their separate ways, back to their homes.

Now Dennis was alone and heading back to the Wilsons' house.

Switchblade Sam was positively gleeful as he followed Dennis. Without Dennis knowing it, he was leading Switchblade Sam directly to the house where all those valuable gold coins were hidden.

Coins that Switchblade Sam would steal the first chance he could!

18.
Garden Party Hijinks

That afternoon, Martha got a call from Alice. The good news was that Alice enjoyed her business trip. The bad news was that her flight had been delayed and she had no idea what time she would be coming home.

Could Dennis stay with the Wilsons longer than planned?

Mr. Wilson was in shock when he heard the news. That evening was the night the flower show would be held in his garden. It was the evening his special plant, the one he had been cultivating for forty years, would bloom for only a few seconds and astound his guests. It was to be the crowning moment in his retired life.

And now he would have to share it with Dennis.

Mr. Wilson tried to figure the chances against Dennis causing trouble at the flower show and ruining his greatest moment.

They weren't very good.

"This is a very important event for me," Mr. Wilson said to Dennis later that evening. They were sitting on the porch waiting for the flower-show committee to arrive. Mr. Wilson was dressed in his best summer suit. Martha was dressed in an attractive floral print dress. Even Dennis was dressed in his Sunday clothes.

"I know," said Dennis.

"I don't want any nonsense," Mr. Wilson warned him. "You mind whatever manners you have and don't make a pest of yourself."

"Okay," agreed Dennis. "Don't drop that stuff, stay off the grass, and don't mess up the flowers!"

Mr. Wilson smiled nervously at Dennis. "Don't embarrass me," he said firmly.

It wasn't long before the members of the Garden Club began to arrive. Mr. Wilson had planned the entire evening around the very second his mock orchid plant was scheduled to bloom. First he would be given the award for being selected as the winner of the Floraganza Competition. Then, while everyone waited for his mock orchid to bloom, he would treat his guests to the extravagant dessert and coffee buffet that Martha had arranged on a picnic table.

And he made special arrangements to keep Dennis as far away from his guests as possible. He made him sit in a chair in front of the garage.

It was close enough for Dennis to be able to see the ceremony, but far enough away so that he couldn't cause mischief.

The garage was right next to the picnic table that had been arranged with rows of delicious desserts. . . .

As Dennis watched the group of elderly Garden Club members file past him onto Mr. Wilson's patio, he leaned back in his chair and began to swing to and fro. Each time he leaned back he got a glimpse of the inside wall of the garage. There was a button on the wall next to the door. It was the button that made the garage door open and close. Dennis had played with such a button often in his own garage.

It was a lot of fun. . . .

Dennis knew that Mr. Wilson might get upset if he pressed the control button and started the garage door opening and closing. He tried to look away from the control button, but it was so tempting. It was just sitting there on the wall waiting to be pressed!

Dennis raised his fingers and slowly brought them closer and closer to the button. His fingers were twitching because he was nervous. What could happen? he wondered. Mr. Wilson is all the way at the other end of the garden. What harm would it do to have a little fun?

SLAM! Dennis smashed his finger down on the button.

Suddenly the wheels and pullies of the garage door began to whirr and turn. Dennis leaped off his chair and out of the way as the huge square door began to rise.

Then Dennis heard a strange rattle coming from the driveway in front of the garage. The bottom of the garage door had clamped itself under the nearest end of the dessert-filled picnic table. Its back legs were being lifted off the ground. The table began to tilt.

Pitchers of cream began to slide down toward the other end of the table. . . .

They were followed by piles of plates and coffee cups, forks, knives, and spoons . . .

. . . by Martha Wilson's scrumptious desserts, too. . . .

Finally, a huge watermelon rolled over everything, off the table, down the driveway, and out onto the street where it was promptly flattened by a passing car. . . .

Oops.

In a short matter of minutes the award ceremony had ended and Mr. Wilson soon held a shiny award plaque in his hands. Everyone was congratulating him, and the photographer from the newspaper was taking his picture. Even Dennis was standing in the crowd applauding Mr. Wilson. He did not want to be seen next to the mess he had just caused at the picnic table. He hoped that maybe Mr. and Mrs. Wilson would think it happened all by itself. That happened sometimes, he thought. Didn't it?

But as soon as the Wilsons led their guests onto the driveway for dessert they could tell what had occurred. All eyes immediately fell on Dennis, who was standing in the garden path with his hands innocently planted in his pockets.

"I made a mistake," said Dennis. He was embarrassed.

In no time at all Dennis was sent to the Wilsons' bedroom where he would have to watch the rest of the garden show from the upstairs window.

19.
Dennis Makes
a Discovery

Dennis watched from the Wilsons' window as all the guests gathered around the patio garden. He felt lonely and left out. In the sky, the huge, silvery full moon burst through some passing clouds. Dennis looked up and made out the features of the face of the man in the moon. The face was smiling, as usual.

Down in the garden Mr. Wilson was directing his guests' attention to his mock orchid. The buds were peeled back and it looked about ready to bloom. Mr. Wilson kept looking at his watch. His greatest moment was almost at hand.

Switchblade Sam spit on the Wilsons' driveway before he snuck into the house through a side window. He couldn't ask for a better setup. The house seemed empty and everybody seemed occupied with some flower show in the back yard.

For Switchblade Sam, the coast was clear for an easy heist.

He moved quickly through the foyer and looked for Mr. Wilson's library. He didn't even bother to walk quietly, since he could not be heard above the sound of the mingling guests out back.

Once he found the library, Switchblade Sam went straight to the bookcase and began looking for the disguised safe about which Dennis had told him. In a matter of minutes he had found it and pried it open with his gloved hands. Inside was Mr. Wilson's coin collection. Switchblade Sam grabbed the coin collection and ran out of the room.

He had finally found what he had come to town for.

Suddenly Dennis heard a door slam shut. The sound came from downstairs in Mr. Wilson's library. He decided to go down and investigate. When he reached the library he was shocked to find a big mess. All of Mr. Wilson's books were strewn about the shelves and floor. His secret safe was wide open and empty.

Mr. Wilson's coin collection was gone!

It had been *stolen!*

Dennis ran out of the library. He had to find Mr. Wilson and tell him that someone had broken into the library and stolen his coin collection. He raced past the foyer and through the kitchen. Then he burst through the kitchen door and out onto the back patio where everybody's attention was focused on Mr. Wilson's mock orchid.

It was just about to bloom when Dennis, at the very top of his lungs, yelled: "MR. WILSON! SOMEBODY ROBBED YOUR HOUSE!"

Everybody jumped out of their seats and turned their heads toward Dennis, just as Mr. Wilson's plant bloomed under the bright light of the moon.

"My plant!" Mr. Wilson shouted at them. He was trying to get their attention.

But by the time everybody turned their heads back to the flower bed, clouds had covered the moon and the petals of the plant began to close.

Soon the plant was completely closed up.

And nobody ever got to see it open.

All because of Dennis.

Oops.

Mr. Wilson screamed. He pushed past his guests, many of whom were still confused and befuddled by all the commotion.

Dennis was standing on the patio when Mr. Wilson reached him. A fearful expression was on his face.

"You're a pest!" Mr. Wilson shouted at him for all to hear. "A menace! A selfish, spoiled, little boy and I have no use for you. You took something from me that I can't get back. Something that means more to me than you ever will. Do you understand?"

Dennis nodded timidly. He was on the verge of tears.

"Outta my way!" said Mr. Wilson coldly. Dennis carefully stepped aside and let Mr. Wilson pass.

Mr. Wilson stormed toward his house.

"Mr. Wilson?" called Dennis. "I'm sorry!"

But Mr. Wilson did not turn back. He just kept on walking until he entered his house and slammed the door behind him.

Mr. Wilson was so embarrassed he told all of his guests to go home early. After they left he started to go upstairs, but ran into Martha on his way up.

"Dennis was telling the truth," Martha told her husband. "There was someone in the house. Your coins were stolen. Nothing's missing upstairs."

"If he hadn't come here in the first place," began Mr. Wilson, "if he didn't live next door, if I'd never seen the brat, none of this would have happened."

"George!" said Martha sternly. She thought Mr. Wilson was being too hard on Dennis.

But Mr. Wilson didn't care what his wife thought. He was just plain too angry to care. "I'm going to bed," he told her. "There isn't much else the little rat can ruin. Wake me up if he sets my car on fire."

"Is Dennis outside?" asked Martha as her husband pushed past her.

"I don't know," growled Mr. Wilson. "And I don't care."

20.
On the Lam

Dennis decided to run away. It was the only thing to do. He had caused so much trouble that he was certain no one would want to see him anymore.

As soon as all of Mr. Wilson's guests had gone, Dennis climbed on his bicycle and rode away. The only thing he took with him was his wagon full of junk. A kid needs a lot of junk when he runs away.

Dennis rode and rode through the streets of his neighborhood and then into the woods. Soon he found himself pedaling faster and faster. He wanted to get as far away from Mr. Wilson's house as possible.

The branches of the trees blocked the moonlight. An owl hooted at Dennis as he rode by. Dennis became frightened. It was very dark in the woods. Dennis was not quite sure where he was headed. He was hoping to find his tree house. He would hide out there until Mr. Wilson cooled down.

Dennis could hardly see in the darkness. He felt the bumpy rocks and mounds beneath the wheels of his bicycle. Behind him his wagon bounced up and down. Suddenly Dennis felt the ground beneath him give way. His bicycle leaped off the crest of a hill and was now falling into a gully. Now Dennis was racing downhill faster than he could pedal.

From somewhere behind him he heard a coyote howl. Dennis looked back fearfully. When he turned his head forward he saw a tall shadow looming in front of him. He shrieked and mashed his feet down on the bicycle pedals. The bicycle finally slid to a screeching stop. Dennis looked up in fear.

It was Switchblade Sam who stood before him.

"We meet again," said Switchblade Sam, exposing his rotted teeth in a grin.

Dennis was relieved. Switchblade Sam was his friend. He felt he could use a friend right about then.

"At first I was really scared because I thought you were a ghost or a killer," Dennis said. He followed Switchblade Sam through the woods. He had no idea that Switchblade Sam was hiding out because he had just stolen Mr. Wilson's coin collection.

"But then I recognized you," continued Dennis. "Now I'm not scared. You got any more of that chocolate?"

"No," said Switchblade Sam.

"Are we going to the tree house?" asked Dennis.

"Nope," said Switchblade Sam.

"You know what?" began Dennis. "I'm running away."

"Good," said Switchblade Sam.

"Yep," continued Dennis. "I caused a bunch of trouble and got yelled at. Old Mr. Wilson really hates me now 'cause I wrecked his party and the greatest moment of his life."

"That's a cryin' shame," said Switchblade Sam, who was only half listening.

"Yep," said Dennis. "And his house got robbed. He's having a really bad night. So, it's probably a good idea that I spend the night with you."

"Yeah," agreed Switchblade Sam with a mischievous grin. "It's gonna work out fine. You can be my hostage."

"Cool," said Dennis, although he had no idea what a hostage was.

Switchblade Sam pulled Dennis along and headed deeper into the woods.

When Alice Mitchell arrived home she was surprised to see so many police cars in the Wilsons' driveway. Her first concern was for Dennis and she immediately asked Martha if he was all right.

It wasn't until after Mr. Wilson reported his stolen coin collection to the police that everyone realized that Dennis was missing. So some officers stayed with Alice, while others went out to look for the boy.

Alice called Joey's mother, but Joey hadn't seen Dennis all day. Alice became very worried. Dennis was nowhere to be found.

Even Mr. Wilson became worried. He was sitting out on his patio and thinking of all the mean things he had said to Dennis. Things like: "Don't you ever come back!" and "Don't make a pest of yourself!" and "I don't ever want to see you again as long as I live!" and, of course, "You're a menace!"

Now Mr. Wilson regretted saying those things to Dennis. He felt responsible for Dennis's running away. He did not even care if the police found his valuable coin collection as long as they found Dennis and returned him home safe and sound.

21.
Dennis the Hostage

"**I** can only be your hostage until tomorrow," said Dennis. "I have church in the morning."

He and Switchblade Sam were sitting beneath a rail bridge, around a small campfire. A small cooking pot hung over the fire.

"You ain't going to church," said Switchblade Sam. "You and me are catching the midnight train outta here."

"We have to stop at my house first," said Dennis quite seriously. "I'll have to tell my mom and dad. Otherwise they'll worry. *And* I have to get new underwear and my camera. *And* I have to tell my mom and dad to feed my fish. *And* I have to get sun block and vitamins and some stuff to play with on the train so I don't get bored."

Switchblade Sam had heard enough. "Put a cork in it," he said impatiently. "You're giving me a headache."

"I don't have a cork," replied Dennis.

"Shut your mouth," insisted Switchblade Sam.

"I can't," said Dennis. "My nose is stuffy because of my allergies and if I shut my mouth I can't breath good."

"Keep your mouth open, but don't talk."

Dennis looked at Switchblade Sam quizzically. "Where do you put a cork when you put a cork in it?" he asked.

"Didn't I ask you to shut your yap?" said Switchblade Sam. He was getting impatient.

"You asked me to shut my mouth," answered Dennis.

"So shut it!"

"What's a yap?"

"It's your mouth!"

Dennis thought about that for a minute. "I can't shut my mouth because my nose is stuffy," he reminded Switchblade Sam.

"SHUT UP!" yelled Switchblade Sam. Then he got up and went over and began to rummage through his duffel bag.

After a moment Dennis tapped Switchblade Sam on the shoulder. "I have one more question," he said.

"What?" said Switchblade Sam with an exasperated grunt.

"What does a hostage have to do?"

"Nothing."

"How come you need one?"

"In case the cops show up," answered Switchblade Sam.

"Do I get to use a gun?" asked Dennis.

Switchblade Sam smiled. "You can stand in front of me," he said, "in case the cops use a gun."

Switchblade Sam had pulled a can of baked beans from his duffel bag and was now opening it with a can opener. Meanwhile Dennis took his slingshot out of his back pocket.

"I got a slingshot," said Dennis proudly.

"Swell," said Switchblade Sam. He couldn't care less.

"I'm a real good shot," said Dennis. "Wanna see?"

Switchblade Sam ignored Dennis and continued to open the can of beans.

Maybe he didn't hear me, thought Dennis. "Excuse me? Mister?" He asked again. "Wanna see?"

But Switchblade Sam, who was apparently very hungry for beans, continued to ignore him.

"Mister? Mister?" asked Dennis insistently. "Can you watch me for a minute?"

Switchblade Sam threw an angry stare at Dennis and then returned to his work.

Dennis decided to show Switchblade Sam his slingshot skills anyway.

"I'll tell you when to look," he said to the kidnapper. Then he took a marble out of his pocket and loaded it into his slingshot. He pulled back the sling, took aim at a tree trunk, and let the marble fly.

"Look!" Dennis shouted.

Switchblade Sam was emptying the can of beans into the cooking pot when he looked up. His eyes widened in alarm. The marble had bounced off the tree and was now heading straight at him!

SMACK! The marble hit Switchblade Sam right in his forehead and knocked him off his feet.

When Dennis saw that Switchblade Sam was lying on his back he walked over to him. "Darn," he sighed. "You missed it."

Dennis put his slingshot back into his pocket. That was when he noticed that the campfire was starting to die down.

"Your fire's getting puny," Dennis called out. "When my dad makes a fire and it gets puny, he wiggles it around and it gets bigger."

Switchblade could not say anything. He was groggy from being hit in the head with the marble. He rolled over and started to pick himself up. His back was to Dennis as he got up on his knees. The seat of his pants had slipped down so that his bottom was exposed.

Dennis was thinking back to last summer when he and his parents went on their annual overnight camping trip. His father had added some twigs to the fire to keep it from going out.

Dennis looked around and picked up a long twig from the ground. Then he stuck it into the shrinking fire and stirred it around, just as he remembered seeing his father do in the past. This caused the embers in the fire to crackle and spark. Soon some of them were flying far out of the campfire itself.

One jumped so high out of the fire that it sailed through the air and landed on Switchblade Sam's exposed behind.

Oops.

Switchblade Sam screamed. He reached around and grabbed his behind. It was burning!

Switchblade Sam began jumping around. He threw himself on the ground, bottom first, and began rolling his burning behind in the dirt, screaming all the while. Then he ran the few feet down to a shallow creek where he sat himself down in the cool water until the pain went away.

He sighed with relief.

When the pain had completely gone, Switch-blade Sam looked up to see Dennis standing at the freshly lit campfire and holding the smoldering twig.

"The fire's bigger now," smiled Dennis proudly.

When Henry Mitchell got out of the taxi that had brought him home from the airport, the first thing he saw were two police cars parked in his driveway.

Grabbing his suitcase, he ran into the house to find Alice sitting in the living room with Martha Wilson and two policemen.

"Alice!" Henry exclaimed in alarm.

He was afraid to ask what had happened.

* * *

113

When he had recovered, Switchblade Sam hung his wet clothes over some bushes to dry. The seat of his long johns was charred and blackened.

He decided he had to do something to keep Dennis from causing any more mischief, so he pulled a rope and a pair of handcuffs out of his duffel bag. Then he turned to Dennis, who was still sitting by the campfire.

"You're finished, pipsqueak," said Switchblade Sam as he approached Dennis with the shackles. "Nobody shoots me in the head with a marble and sets my pants on fire."

"It was an accident," pleaded Dennis.

"There ain't gonna be no more accidents," snarled Switchblade Sam. "Turn around!"

Dennis obediently turned away and stood patiently as Switchblade Sam started to tie the rope around his ankles. Dennis looked down at the way Switchblade Sam was wrapping the rope.

"You're doing it wrong," Dennis told him. "I had a baby-sitter once who tied me up like that. I took my shoes off and I was out."

"Get lost," replied Switchblade Sam looking at his handiwork. "I tied up lots of guys in my life."

"Okay," said Dennis. "I bet you never tied up a five-year-old. I'll just get away."

"I'll make this rope so tight, you won't be able to move."

Dennis shrugged. "The rope's too big and my

legs are too small to make it tight enough," he explained. "There's only one way to do it and I know because lots of people have tried to tie me up. It doesn't work. But you try your way. I'll get out and you'll just have to keep doing it."

Switchblade Sam stopped tying the rope. Something about what Dennis was saying made good sense.

"What do you do different?" he asked the boy.

Dennis took the rope away from Switchblade Sam. "Sit down," he said.

"I can't," said Switchblade Sam, remembering the pain in his bottom.

"It's okay," said Dennis. "I'll do it standing up."

And with that Dennis began to wrap the rope around one of Switchblade Sam's ankles. He made a loop and pulled it tight. Then he began to loop the rope around the other ankle.

"You gotta tie each foot up by itself," he explained as he went along. "Then you tie them together."

Switchblade Sam looked down at his ankles. He was paying strict attention to the way Dennis was securing the rope. Soon each of his ankles was tied together, joined by a double width of rope.

"No matter how much I wiggle," said Dennis, "I can't get out. Tight, huh?"

"Yeah," said Switchblade Sam as he struggled to break free from the rope.

"Then if you really don't want me to move at

115

all," said Dennis as he picked up the set of handcuffs from the ground, "put one hand behind your back."

Switchblade Sam put one hand behind his back.

"Bend down," ordered Dennis.

Switchblade Sam bent down. Dennis stepped around him. He made sure Switchblade Sam's hands were hanging between his legs and through the width of the rope. Then he clamped the handcuffs around Switchblade Sam's wrists until they were locked tight.

Switchblade Sam was now unable to straighten up from his bent-over position.

"You could untie the ropes with your hands," said Switchblade Sam.

Dennis shook his head no. "I'm not done," he said. He reached into Switchblade Sam's duffel bag and pulled out a roll of silver duct tape.

"Instead of putting this on my mouth," he said as he tore off a length of the tape, "which you can't because I have a stuffy nose, you — " and he began wrapping Switchblade Sam's hands with the tape. When he was done he took a step back and looked at his handiwork.

"You can't get out of that at all, right?" Dennis asked Switchblade Sam.

Switchblade Sam struggled to break free of the bonds, but with no success. "Nope," he answered.

"I told you," said Dennis. "You tie me up like that and I can't ever, ever get out."

116

"Thanks," said Switchblade Sam. "Let me loose now."

"Okay," said Dennis.

"Get the handcuff key."

"Where is it?"

"It's next to my knife."

Dennis looked around and saw Switchblade Sam's switchblade sitting on a rock. Next to it was a small silver handcuff key. Dennis was pleased with himself for finding the key. With a smile he turned to bring it to Switchblade Sam, but his foot tripped against the rock and he went stumbling to the ground.

The handcuff key flew out of his hand and landed in the bean pot, which was still cooking over the campfire.

The key sank deep into the simmering beans. Oops.

Mr. Wilson felt so bad about Dennis's disappearance that he went for a long drive by himself. After a while he found himself parked in front of the town church. He got out of his car and stood in front of the church, looking helplessly up at the cross atop its roof.

"Excuse me," Mr. Wilson said to the cross. "Listen, if you give me a hand, I'd appreciate it."

Mr. Wilson looked at the cross for a long time. He prayed for a miracle to find Dennis. Then he drove off to look for him, alone.

22.
Who Kidnapped Whom?

Dennis knew there was only one way to get to the handcuff key at the bottom of the bean pot: He would have to empty the pot. But Dennis also knew it wasn't right to throw away food. So he began to feed Switchblade Sam spoonfuls of beans.

He fed him.

And fed him.

And fed him.

Until Switchblade Sam's belly looked as if it were about to burst.

When the bean pot was empty, Dennis looked inside, but he did not find the handcuff key.

"Uh-oh," Dennis said to Switchblade Sam. "You must have swallowed it."

"You little worm!" yelled Switchblade Sam, his mouth full of beans.

"I swallowed my allowance once," said Dennis. "I had to wait a whole night and day to get it back."

The next thing they knew the campfire had almost gone out. Dennis went on a search for firewood. He found a huge two-foot-long chunk on the railroad bridge, which was right over their campsite.

"IF YOU WEREN'T SO CRABBY, THIS WOULD BE LIKE A CAMPING TRIP!" he yelled down to Switchblade Sam, who was still tied up in a big human knot.

Dennis lifted the chunk of wood onto the bridge railing. "FIREWOOD!" he called out, pushing the wood over the side of the bridge. "BOMBS AWAY!"

Switchblade Sam looked up just in time to see the chunk of wood hurling down — right onto his head!

He was knocked out cold.

When Dennis climbed back down to the campfire he looked at the unconscious Switchblade Sam. He looked like he was sleeping.

"Poor little lamb," said Dennis. "He must be exhausted. I better cover him up so he doesn't catch his death of cold."

Dennis went over to Switchblade Sam's things and began to unroll the blanket that lay next to the duffel bag. At the same time, Switchblade Sam began to regain consciousness. He rose up on his knees and then to his feet, but he was still hunched over and shackled by the rope, the handcuffs, and the duct tape.

Dennis unrolled the blanket with such force that some of the items that had been tucked inside it came flying out. One was the jewelry box that Switchblade Sam had stolen from the house with the open window.

The jewelry box hurled through the air until it landed with a *thud* — right on Switchblade Sam's head. Switchblade Sam toppled over — unconscious again.

Next, Dennis unfurled the blanket the rest of the way. He did not notice that one end of the blanket passed through the campfire. By the time he covered Switchblade Sam with it, the blanket was starting to smolder and smoke.

When Switchblade Sam was all tucked in, Dennis picked up the jewelry box and went to put it in the duffel bag for safe keeping. But when he opened the duffel bag and looked inside, he was surprised to find a woman's purse there.

"What's he got a purse for?" Dennis wondered aloud.

He opened the purse and found it filled with wallets. Lots of them. And each wallet was stuffed with cash.

"Holy smokes!" exclaimed Dennis. "He's rich!"

Suddenly Dennis began to sniff the air. Something smelled funny. Like something was burning. He turned around and saw that the blanket he had covered Switchblade Sam with had now burst into flames!

Just then Switchblade Sam opened his eyes and saw that he was on fire!

Dennis grabbed the duffel bag, which was filled with all kinds of heavy canned foods and eating utensils, and slammed it down on Switchblade Sam to put out the flames.

That hurt Switchblade Sam.

And although the flames died out, Switchblade Sam was knocked out cold. Again.

Henry and Alice Mitchell had been sitting out on the Wilsons' porch for several hours. Martha was sitting with them. They were exhausted with worry. Both Mr. Wilson and the police had gone out looking for Dennis. As yet, no one had returned from the search.

Then Mr. Wilson pulled up in his car and got out. He walked over to the Mitchells with a forlorn expression on his face.

"I couldn't find him," said Mr. Wilson shaking his head.

He climbed up onto the porch to face Alice and Henry. "This is my fault," he admitted to them. "I'm sorry."

"It's not your fault," said Alice. "I shouldn't have gone away. I shouldn't have gone back to work."

"That's not the cause, Alice," interrupted Mr. Wilson. "It's me. I hurt Dennis. I said some terrible things to him. Things that no man should

121

ever say to a child. Hurtful, destructive things."

"We'll find him, George," said Henry. "You don't have to feel that way."

Mr. Wilson took a thoughtful pause and sighed. "I'll tell you something I never told anybody," he said. "Something I never knew until tonight. I can't be nice to the little bugger because I'm too ashamed to admit — that I love him."

Martha looked up at her husband, startled by his admission. She smiled at him. She knew he cared for Dennis all the time, but was just too stubborn to admit it. His saying so made her love Mr. Wilson all the more.

"If anything happens to him," said Mr. Wilson as tears welled in his eyes, "I'll never forgive myself."

23.
The Truth About
Switchblade Sam

That night, the town was lit up by hundreds of flashlights. And each flashlight was held by a person who was looking for Dennis.

Henry roamed the streets in search of his son. He was exhausted.

Joey aimed his flashlight down all the sewers hoping to find some sign of his best pal.

Even Polly had summoned all the baby-sitters in town to search for the boy for whom they dreaded to sit.

Margaret sat at home and stared out the window. She was on the verge of tears. "I've lost the only man I've ever loved," she sighed aloud.

Badly bruised, with charred skin and burnt hair, Switchblade Sam slowly rose out of the creek. Despite the cool freshness of the water, he was still smoldering from being set on fire.

The only problem was that Switchblade Sam could not get out of the creek. His ankles were still tied with rope and his wrists were still shackled by handcuffs. As a result, he was having a hard time regaining his balance.

Dennis was climbing the trestle of the railroad embankment with a block and tackle and rope that he had found in Switchblade Sam's duffel bag. He couldn't figure out why Switchblade Sam needed so much rope, but he was glad it was there. Otherwise, how could he help his friend out of the creek?

"I'll get you outta there," Dennis shouted from the bridge. "You shouldn't jump in a river with handcuffs on, for gosh sakes! You could drown."

Climbing a mail-pouch holder, he hooked the block and tackle around its arm.

"It's a good thing I know a lot about ropes, huh?" Dennis called out to his drenched friend.

The water had loosened the tape that bound Switchblade Sam's wrists and the fire had burned the rope from his ankles. Now Switchblade Sam was bending over in the water and reaching toward the shore. His knife, which had been thrown during all the confusion, was lying almost within reach. He wanted to get it before Dennis returned.

"When I get you out, I'm going to sleep," called Dennis as he headed toward the river unraveling the rope behind him. "I'm beat. It must be all this fresh air."

Switchblade Sam could not reach the knife. And by now Dennis had reached the edge of the river.

"Lift up your arms so I can put the lasso over you," Dennis ordered. Switchblade Sam raised his arms. He grabbed the rope as it dropped over him.

Dennis pulled at the rope, struggling to help Switchblade Sam out of the river. But as he did this, he looked down to see a shiny gold coin on the ground. Next to it was another gold coin. Next to that one was another . . . and another . . . and another.

The coins must have fallen out of Switchblade Sam's bedroll, thought Dennis. He bent over and picked up some of them. He studied them for a moment until he realized:

"This is Mr. Wilson's gold," he said to Switchblade Sam. "How come you got it?"

Switchblade Sam had risen out of the creek and pulled himself onto the embankment. "I stole it," he said with a sneaky grin.

Dennis's eyes opened wide. "You're a robber?" he asked.

"I'm a robber," replied Switchblade Sam. He had retrieved his knife and now popped it open for Dennis to see.

Dennis swallowed with fear. "Uh-oh," he said.

Switchblade Sam had had enough of the little menace and decided to get rid of him.

Switchblade Sam was so intent on getting Dennis out of his hair that he never took the tackle rope from around his chest. The other end of the rope was still attached to the mail-pouch holder, which stood right next to the train tracks.

Just about then, a train whistle could be heard in the distance. A train was coming around the bend.

But Switchblade Sam was so angry he didn't notice the approaching train.

"Say your prayers, little rat," scowled Switchblade Sam as he aimed his knife at Dennis.

"I can't," replied Dennis in a weak voice. He was scared. "I didn't take my bath yet."

"Have it your way," grinned Switchblade Sam and raised the knife higher.

Dennis covered his eyes, fearing the worst.

Just then the train whizzed by overhead. As it passed the mail-pouch holder, it snagged the rope Dennis had tied there to save Switchblade Sam from the river.

Through his fingers, Dennis could see the train grab the rope. He uncovered his eyes and looked at Switchblade Sam, grinning.

Switchblade Sam wondered what Dennis had to grin about, since he was still holding a knife over the boy's head. Then he, too, looked up.

He saw the train.

He saw the train pulling the rope.

He followed the rope with his eye until he found the other end of it.

The other end that was attached to *him!*

No wonder Dennis was smiling.

Suddenly, Switchblade Sam grew frantic. He could see the rope ahead of him unraveling. Soon he would be pulled and dragged by the huge, fast train. He desperately tried to saw through the rope with his knife, but it was too late.

Switchblade Sam was ripped off his feet. The rope rocketed him up off the bank and under the railroad bridge. His knife went flying out of his hand and landed in a crack on the underside of the bridge, where it remained hanging.

WHAM! Switchblade Sam slammed into the underside of the bridge — and stuck there!

The train continued to pull the rope until the tension became so great that the rope snapped.

Switchblade Sam slowly began to slide off the underside of the railroad bridge. He opened his eyes and looked down. He was starting to fall. He clawed and scratched at the bridge, but to no avail.

It was a long fall. And Switchblade Sam screamed all the way down.

He crash-landed, face first, in an old skiff that was sitting in the creek. The boat broke to bits upon his impact.

Delirious, Switchblade Sam looked up from the creek. Something was falling toward him. As it got closer he could make out that it was square shaped, like a block. Switchblade Sam gulped with dread. It was the block and tackle! The same block and tackle he had used many times when robbing houses. It was now heading down at him at a ferocious speed. He covered his head, but with no success.

The block and tackle beaned him. He rolled over, and groaned in pain.

Dennis climbed down to the creek and looked at the unconscious robber.

"Oh, boy," he said. "He's gonna have a headache. I better get him an aspirin."

Dennis took out his sling shot. After all, it was the best way he knew to feed someone an aspirin.

Meanwhile, Switchblade Sam floated, face down, to the river bank. He was exhausted and beaten. He figured the worst was behind him.

But he didn't see his knife, which was still stuck in the underside of the railroad bridge. It came loose and slipped out.

It hurtled downward.

Straight downward.

Point first.

Right toward Switchblade Sam's behind.

Dennis looked up at the sound of Switchblade Sam's scream. Maybe, he thought, he ought to feed him *two* aspirins.

24.
And the Winner Is . . .

The hours ticked by with no sign of Dennis. Alice and Henry finally fell asleep in their living room. In another chair, even the Police Chief was snoozing.

Mr. Wilson had remained out on the porch. He was wide awake. Every time he heard a sound he looked up and down his front lane, hoping that it was Dennis returning home safe and sound.

But it never was.

Eventually some police officers came upon the area beneath the railroad bridge where Dennis and Switchblade Sam had made camp. But by now the thief and the boy were gone.

In fact, the only sign the police could find of Dennis was his stuffed teddy bear, abandoned in the dirt.

The police felt hopeless and left the area. They returned to the Mitchells' house with the sad news that they had no luck in finding Dennis. But they would not give up. They would try again in the morning.

By morning, Mr. Wilson had fallen asleep on the porch swing. He was awakened by a loud thud in the bushes. Dennis? he hoped. But when he went to investigate all he found was the morning paper that had been thrown by the paper boy.

Mr. Wilson tucked the paper under his arm and turned to climb back onto the porch. As he turned, he thought he heard something down the road. He cupped his hand to his ear and listened carefully.

Nothing. He was mistaken. He continued toward the porch stairs.

Suddenly he thought he heard something again. This time he turned around to face the street.

Some cats scattered for cover.

Some squirrels scampered hurriedly up a tree.

A gopher squirted down a hole in his front yard.

Then came the sound Mr. Wilson was waiting for. The scraping, jangling, rattling, and grinding of a speeding bicycle.

Dennis's bicycle!

"Martha!" Mr. Wilson called out. "Alice! Henry!"

Seconds later, Mr. Wilson saw Dennis wobbling down the street on his bicycle, pulling his wagon close behind. In the wagon, handcuffed, and roped, was a disheveled-looking Switchblade Sam.

"Hey, Mr. Wilson!" called Dennis as he brought his bicycle to a screeching halt on the Wilsons' front lane.

Switchblade Sam looked up from the wagon to see where he was. He was a sorry-looking prisoner. "Help," he pleaded to anyone who would hear him.

Mr. Wilson fell to his knees and held his arms wide open when he saw Dennis. Happy tears welled in his eyes. Dennis climbed off of his bicycle and ran to Mr. Wilson. They gave each other a big, warm hug.

"Guess what?" said Dennis holding out the bag with Mr. Wilson's coin collection. "I got your gold back!"

Mr. Wilson smiled. "I'm just glad to have you back," he told Dennis. "I don't care about the gold."

Dennis furrowed his brow. "Really? Can I have it?" he asked.

Within seconds Alice, Henry, and Martha had come from their houses and were rushing toward Dennis with open arms.

Soon Dennis was being smothered with hugs and kisses.

"Sweetheart, where've you been?" asked Alice in between hugs.

"I caught the robber," answered Dennis pointing to his wagon.

Everyone looked over to the wagon. Sure

enough, there was Switchblade Sam, all tied up and unable to move.

"Help," he cried out again.

Soon the Police Chief emerged from the Mitchells' house, stretching and yawning from spending the night in the easy chair. When he saw Switchblade Sam all tied up, he called for some police cars to take the robber away.

"You can tell everybody in the big house that you met our Dennis Mitchell," the police chief told Switchblade Sam gleefully.

Switchblade Sam growled and let himself be taken away.

By now the whole neighborhood had heard of Dennis's triumphant return. A gaggle of kids on bikes raced to the Wilsons' house, where they gathered around Dennis and welcomed him home. Joey led the charge.

When Dennis saw the police taking Switchblade Sam away he suddenly remembered something important. He ran to the police car.

"Mister," he said to Switchblade Sam. "You forgot something."

Dennis reached into his pocket and pulled out a knife. Switchblade Sam's knife. Then he handed it to Switchblade Sam. Switchblade Sam grinned with glee. By using his knife he would be able to make good an escape from the police.

But just then a police officer closed the car door right on Switchblade Sam's cuffed hands. The knife went flying from his hands and out onto the street, where it bounced and dropped down a sidewalk sewer.

The knife was gone forever.

And in a few minutes, so was Switchblade Sam.

Dennis watched as the police car carrying Switchblade Sam drove away. He was positively safe from danger, he thought.

That's when he turned around and came face to face with Margaret Wade.

"I'm overwhelmed with joy that you're not completely killed and gone forever, Dennis," said Margaret.

"Thanks," said Dennis cautiously. He realized he wasn't so safe from danger after all.

"After staying up almost all night and losing a ton of beauty sleep," said Margaret, "I decided that of all the gross and weird boys in the neighborhood, you're the one that I love the most."

"Oh, no," groaned Dennis.

"Yep," said Margaret. "So let's get this thing over with."

The next thing Dennis knew, Margaret had closed her eyes and puckered her lips for a kiss.

Dennis didn't wait. He spun around on his heels and charged into his house, raced up the stairs, and slid under his bed . . .

. . . where he hoped he would finally be safe and sound.

25.
Once a Menace . . .

That evening, after Dennis had been given a much needed bath, his parents took him next door for one of Mr. Wilson's special barbecue dinners. It was a celebration dinner, in honor of Dennis's coming home safe and sound.

After dinner, Alice, Henry, Martha, and Mr. Wilson sat in the patio chairs having coffee. Dennis was standing at the grill roasting a big, fluffy marshmallow. He had placed the marshmallow on the tip of a barbecue prong and was passing it back and forth through a flame.

"The good news," announced Alice to the others, "is I'm not going to have to travel anymore. They want me to stay with the project here. And they agreed to start a day-care program at the office. So, I can take Dennis with me to work."

"That's ridiculous," said Mr. Wilson. "What the heck's he gonna do all day? Don't be foolish. We're right next door. We can watch him."

134

"We'd love to," added Martha.

By now Dennis's marshmallow had become charcoal black. Still, he wasn't sure if it was ready to eat. So he continued to rotate it in the barbecue flame. In fact, he kept cooking it for so long that it soon caught on fire.

"You have to remember back to all the times Dennis upset you," Henry said to Mr. Wilson as the grown-ups continued their discussion. As yet they were unaware of Dennis's flaming marshmallow. They also didn't see as Dennis began whipping the marshmallow back and forth, trying to blow the flame out.

Or how it began to slip off the edge of the barbecue prong . . .

Oops.

Mr. Wilson brushed the notion aside with a wave of his hand. "This is a new ballgame," he said. "I've learned a few things. Kids are kids. They play by their own rules. If you can't buy that, you're looking for trouble. You have to roll with the punches. You have to expect the unexpected."

Just then, and quite unexpectedly, Mr. Wilson looked up to see Dennis's flaming marshmallow come hurtling toward him at top speed. *SMACK!* It landed right in the middle of his forehead and stuck there.

That was when, just as everyone expected, Mr. Wilson began to scream.

26.
. . . Always a Menace

Alice's coworker Andrea was working at the copy machine when she felt someone watching her. She looked from one side to the other, but saw no one. Then she looked down and saw Dennis.

"Aren't you supposed to be in the day-care area with the other children?" she asked him.

"That's where I was," explained Dennis, "but I had to leave because the lady who watches the kids said if she had to look at me for five more seconds, she'd jump out the window. She's a pretty nice lady so I wouldn't want her to do that. What're you copying?"

"A lease for a toy store," answered Andrea.

"My mom says if you put toy stores up on top of a mall, parents gotta go through all the other floors — "

"Would you please leave me alone?" asked Andrea insistently. "I have work to do."

"Can I push the button?" asked Dennis.

"You don't know which button to push," said Andrea as she placed her document to be copied in the machine. Just then the edge of her scarf touched the paper feeder.

Dennis studied the control panel. "It's this one," he said and pressed the button.

Suddenly the machine turned on. The edge of Andrea's scarf was sucked into the paper feeder. Andrea's head snapped forward and landed on the copy glass. She screamed and fumbled with the controls in an attempt to free herself from the machine.

A photocopy of Andrea's face popped out of the copy machine.

Finally, Andrea's scarf tore off her neck. She keeled over and fell on the floor.

As she lay there all she could think of was what she would do to Dennis when she found him. Finding him, she realized, would not be very hard. She could already hear the other workers in the office screaming.

She smiled to herself. All she would have to do is follow the screams. . . .